# The GUITAR SCALE Picture Book

Don Latarski

Alfred Publishing Co., Inc.
16320 Roscoe Blvd., Suite 100
P.O. Box 10003
Van Nuys, CA 91410-0003
alfred.com

ISBN-10: 0-7390-5352-3
ISBN-13: 978-0-7390-5352-2

Cover photographs:
Martin Dreadnought courtesy of Martin Guitars
Back cover photo by Brian Lanker, courtesy of Don Latarski
High resolution textured stationery paper © istock.com/billnoll

# Contents

# Contents

## Professional Highlights

## Don Latarski, guitarist/composer/educator

Don Latarski is known internationally as a gifted performer, composer, and author. His recordings include: *Haven, Lifeline, Private Affair, How Many Ways, NorthWest of December, Deep Play, Rue 2, Natural Instincts, Eden Hall Sessions, Fab 4 on 6, Fab 4 on 6 vol.2, Rue D'Acoustic, Guitars on Holiday, Nightingale* (with vocalist Marilyn Keller), *TUO* (with guitarist John Stowell), and *Acoustica Funkus.*

His numerous publications include: *Introduction to Chord Theory, Scale Patterns for Guitar, Movable Guitar Chords, Arpeggios for Guitar, Chord Orbits, Chord Embellishments, Practical Theory for Guitar, Guitar Theory Basics, The Ultimate Guitar Chord Big Book, Blues Chords, Jazz Chords, First Chords, Barre Chords, Blues Guitar, The Ultimate Guitar Chord Gig Bag Book,* and *The Guitar Scale Picture Book.*

His first instrument was accordion, but he wisely switched to guitar at the age of 10.

Versatility in many contemporary styles has kept him in demand as a performer, session artist, composer, producer and educator. He specializes in finger-style jazz, blues and Americana styles.

Latarski is also adjunct instructor and head of guitar studies at the University of Oregon School of Music and Dance. He's been a faculty member at the university since 1984.

## Acknowledgments:

This book was gracefully nudged along by invaluable contributions from: Kathy Kifer, Aaron Stang, Jack Allen, and Brian Lanker. I do appreciate all they have done along the way.

BRIAN LANKER

# INTRODUCTION

Every aspiring improviser needs a wide variety of scales and modes. It's no longer enough to just know the minor pentatonic. Contemporary musicians are now using the modes of the major, jazz minor, and harmonic minor scales. In addition, blues, pentatonic, diminished, whole tone, and hybrid scales are also frequently heard. This book is a collection of the most common scales in use today.

There are many good reasons for learning a variety of scales: The study of scales can provide a good way to enhance speed, promote economy of movement, extend reach, fluidity, interval relationships, fingerboard logic, and picking technique. Scales are also a great way to develop a wide palate of soloing resources, which can be called upon to create melodies and solos over a wide variety of chord types.

All of the scales in this book are presented in several ways: in picture form on the fingerboard, in TAB form, and in theoretical form. Most people will use the picture/TAB forms. These forms provide instant access to all scales for all keys over the entire fingerboard. If you have a background in music theory, you'll appreciate the information that accompanies each scale at the top of the page.

Every scale is made up of at least five different notes. Two scales have eight-notes; these are the diminished scales. The normal number of notes found in scales is seven. All scales are constructed from the chromatic scale. This scale is made up of 12 different pitches, each a half-step apart. The half-step is the smallest musical distance possible between two notes (without bending). Starting from C, this scale would have the following pitches: C-C#-D-D#-E-F-F#-G-G#-A-A#-B. Every scale or mode in this book is made up of some combination of these pitches.

Each of these 12 pitches is used as the *root* note for 18 different scales and modes. You can think of each of these notes as a key.

One possible source of confusion when looking up a scale comes from the fact that music theory recognizes two different names for some notes that sound exactly the same. For example, C# sounds the same as Db, F# sounds the same as Gb, G# sounds the same as Ab, and A# sounds the same as Bb. These are the common *enharmonic equivalents*. The reason for this seemingly confusing system comes from how notes are spelled in different keys. Each major key must use all seven letters of the musical alphabet. Since this alphabet is made up of A, B, C, D, E, F and G, each scale (unless it has more or less than seven notes), must use one of each of these seven pitches. Bear in mind that each of these note names can be altered to be either a sharped or flatted note. From a practical point of view, if you are trying to find a scale that starts on Db, you may have to look in the C# section of this book. Scales are named and spelled by their most common keys. As an example, the key of Eb is much more common than D#. The scale patterns for C# will be the same as for Db.

The first description of a scale is shown at the top of each page. This series of numbers is called the *scale formula*. The scale formula indicates how a scale or mode deviates from a major scale. For example, the scale formula for a major scale is: 1-2-3-4-5-6-7. If we use C as our beginning root note, the notes are: C-D-E-F-G-A-B. In the key of A major, the notes would be: A-B-C#-D-E-F#-G#. The formula for A major is still 1-2-3-4-5-6-7. Confused? There's another way of describing the major scale. We can do it by looking at the musical distance between each note. In all major scales (it doesn't matter what the key is) the half-steps occur between the 3rd and 4th scales degrees and the 7th and 8th. (The 8th scale degree is the same as the 1st and is not a new note, but just a repetition of the 1st scale degree.) The distance between all other scale degrees is a whole-step. This relationship is expressed with the formula: 1-2-3-4-5-6-7-(8).

$$
\begin{array}{c}
\text{W = whole step} \\
\text{h = half step}
\end{array}
\qquad
\begin{array}{ccccccc}
\text{W} & \text{W} & \text{h} & \text{W} & \text{W} & \text{W} & \text{h} \\
1 - 2 - 3 - 4 - 5 - 6 - 7 - (8)
\end{array}
$$

The scale formula 1-2-♭3-4-5-♭6-♭7 indicates that there are three notes which have been altered from their "normal" major scale order. We'd describe this scale as having a flatted 3rd, 6th and 7th. The name given to this scale is natural minor or Aeolian mode.

If you are a beginner, you may not have any interest in this type of information. At some point in your musical evolution, you will encounter musicians who do understand the meaning and significance of this type of knowledge. This descriptive method also applies to chords and arpeggios. If you are interested in a fuller understanding of this and other theory concepts as they relate to the guitar, check out my book called *Practical Theory for Guitar*.

Directly below the theoretical description of each scale is a list of the actual note names that make up the scale. As mentioned earlier, these note names will be only for the most common keys. Since the key of A♭ is more common that G♯, the notes in the different scales will be referenced to the key of A♭.

The reason for the patterns in this book is based around what is most commonly referred to as the CAGED system. CAGED refers to five different common chord shapes. Most guitarists know these shapes. Note the location of the root notes in each of these shapes. These are shown as solid dots in each chord form. In the C chord, the root tones are located on strings 2 and 5. The A chord has roots on strings 3 and 5. The G chord has roots on 1, 3, and 6. The E chord has roots on 1, 4, and 6. And the D chord has root notes on strings 2 and 4.

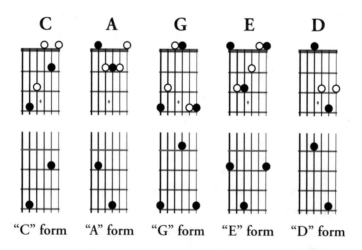

"C" form     "A" form     "G" form     "E" form     "D" form

These CAGED chord forms can be moved around on the fingerboard to produce different voicings for the same chord. For example, it is possible to play an A♭ major chord using these same forms.

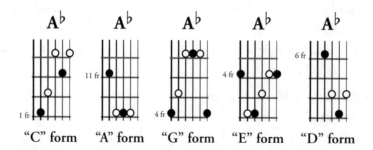

"C" form     "A" form     "G" form     "E" form     "D" form

Each of these CAGED forms contains one or more octave shapes. These octave shapes form the basis for building the scales in this book. One distinct advantage to using this system lies in the fact that most scale patterns don't require a huge hand stretch. In other words, each scale is restricted to as few frets as possible. Here is the G major scale using CAGED shapes.

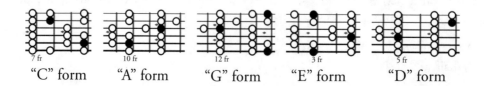

"C" form     "A" form     "G" form     "E" form     "D" form

This isn't the only way of structuring scale patterns on the fingerboard. One of the downsides to building scales based on the CAGED system lies in the fact that some strings may only have two notes on any one string. (If you are really interested in building speed and you absolutely want to pick each note, then you should explore a system of scales where three notes are played on each string.) This system will result in more efficient picking, but your fretting hand will be very stretched out. Of course it is possible to learn both systems and see which one works best for your needs.

The common modes are also found in this book. What distinguishes a mode from a scale is in how the notes in a scale are ordered. The C major scale consists of these notes: C-D-E-F-G-A-B-C. When these notes are played in this order our ears interpret the sound as happy, cheerful, upbeat and pleasant. Why this is so is based upon how our brains interpret sound. First of all, our brains hear a series of notes based upon how this series is ordered. If the above scale notes are played by starting and ending on C notes, then our brain recognizes the C note as the root note (also called the *tonic* in music theory) and all of the intervals produced are referenced to this note. By starting and ending on C, certain interval sounds are produced, namely the major interval between the C note and the E note, and another major interval between the C note and the B note. These intervals define the essence of the major scale sound and are responsible for the "happy and uplifting" sound of this group of notes.

A mode is created whenever the notes of any scale are reordered to create a sense of a new root note, or tonic. If the same notes of the C major scale are shifted so that the starting and ending notes are D (D-E-F-G-A-B-C-D), then our brain perceives this sequence in a very different way. The resulting emotional response is not quite so happy and upbeat due to the intervals that result from the root note. From this lowest note, a couple of minor intervals are produced: a minor 3rd (from D to F) and a minor 7th (from D to C). The formula for this mode is: $1-2-{}^{\flat}3-4-5-6-{}^{\flat}7$. It is known as the Dorian mode. Dorian mode is constructed from the notes of a *parent* major scale. The D Dorian mode is thus contained within the C major scale. It is therefore possible to extract six different modes from each seven-note scale. The most common parent scales from which modes are derived are: the major scale, harmonic minor, jazz minor, diminished, and major pentatonic. Not all modes are equally useful from an improvisatory perspective, so only the most common ones are shown. From this point, the term scale will be used to include all modes as well.

All scales are accompanied with a brief suggestion as to how you might use them for constructing solos or melodies. As all scales have a root note, the primary application of a scale will be tied to the root note of the chord. As an example, a G major scale would sound great when played over a Gmaj7 chord. There are other uses for the G major scale, such as over a G, G6, Gadd9, Gsus2, G5, or G6/9 chords. (See the end of this introduction for a list of suggested scale and chord relationships.)

## HOW TO USE THIS BOOK

When learning a new scale, begin by studying and practicing the individual patterns. Pay particular attention to the root notes in each of the patterns. I usually start by playing about half of the pattern. This spans an octave. I also strongly urge you to record a chord or series of chord vamps, which you can hear while trying to get the scale in your fingers and ear. You need to be training your ear as well as your fingers when learning new scale and mode sounds. If you're going to practice the Dorian sound, lay down some min6, min7, min9 and min11 chords or program them into your sequencer. (If you're going for the C Dorian mode, make sure all of the roots to the above chords are also C.)

I always learn how to play the finger pattern across the fingerboard, then I start connecting two patterns; running back and forth from one to the other, working out appropriate finger shifts. Then I begin building runs that span three or more patterns. I also always try to be musical when the guitar is in my hands. This goes for practicing scales too. I play them with feeling and intent. I don't sit in front of the TV and practice. I concentrate on what I'm doing and do it intensely for short periods of time.

There are always alternate ways of fingering anything and this goes for scales too. You may find a number of alternate fingerings. Explore them all. Different fingerings will result in new musical ideas and sounds. Play these scales in any way you can imagine. Experiment with different rhythmic groupings such as eighth notes, sixteenth notes, triplets and the like. There are many different exercises you can invent which will promote facility with the patterns. Playing the patterns in 3rds, 4ths, 5ths and 6ths is also a good way to develop some new ideas as well as your cross-picking chops. Use hammer-ons, pull-offs, slides and bends too. I'd recommend playing the scales with a clean tone to insure that your accuracy is together before going to the effects.

The biggest challenge to scale playing is in bridging the gap between scales and music. All too often, the playing of scales turns into a boring exercise. This is mindless practicing and might even be a waste of time. The real danger here lies in the fact that you might be having a very negative experience with something that should be uplifting and positive. This kind of experience does little to promote creativity and experimentation. When the scales become tedious and boring, stop and give yourself a break. Do something more enjoyable. Set a pace for yourself that is ambitious yet attainable.

Lastly, I suggest learning the major scale and its modes first. These are by far the most important patterns. Next, learn the blues and pentatonic scales (if you're into rock and blues). If you're into jazz, make sure you know the jazz minor and harmonic minor scale modes (in addition to the major scale and its modes as well as the blues scale). You'll also find that the diminished (both versions) and the whole-tone scales are helpful.

Chords can be written in a variety of ways. There is no one, absolute standard. Here are some of the most common ways of writing major, minor, dominant, and diminished chords. Each of these chords will be notated with C as the root tone. Suggested scale/mode choices are indicated.

C = major triad

Csus2 = major triad with a 2nd substituting for the chordal 3rd

C6, Cma6 = major triad with added 6th

C6/9, C6sus2, C6(add9) = major 6th with added 9th

Cma7, Cmaj7, CM7, C△7, C7 = major triad with added 7th

C6/7, Cma6/7 = major 6th with added 7th

Cma7($\flat$5), Cmaj7(-5), C△7($\flat$5), C7($\flat$5) = major 7th with a lowered 5th

C(9), C(add9) = major triad with an added 9th

Cma9, Cmaj9, C△9 = major 7th with added 9th

Cma9($\flat$5), Cmaj9(-5), C△9($\flat$5) = major 9th with a lowered 5th

Cma9($\sharp$11), Cmaj7($\sharp$11), CM7(+11), C△7($\sharp$11), C7(+11) = major 7th with a raised 11th

---

Cm, Cmi, Cmin, C- = minor triad

Cm6, Cmi6, Cmin6, C-6 = minor triad with added 6th

Cm6/7, Cmi6/7, Cmin6/7 = minor 7th with an added 6th

Cm7, Cmi7, Cmin7, C-7 = minor triad with lowered 7th

Cm7($\sharp$5), Cmi7(+5), Cmin7($\sharp$5), C-7($\sharp$5) = minor 7th with a raised 5th

Cm7($\flat$5), Cm7(-5), Cmi7($\flat$5), Cmi7(-5), Cmin7($\flat$5), Cmin7(-5), C$^{\emptyset}$ = minor 7th with a lowered 5th

Cm($\sharp$7), Cmi($\sharp$7), Cmin($\sharp$7), Cm($\natural$7) = minor triad with an added natural 7th

Cm(add9), Cmi(add 9), Cmin(add9), Cm(9) = minor triad chord with an added 9th

Cm9, Cmi9, Cmin9, C-9 = minor 7th chord with an added 9th

Cm11, Cmi11, Cmin11, C-11 = minor 9th chord with an added 11th

Cm13, Cmi13, Cmin13, C-13 = minor 11th chord with an added 13th

C7 = major triad with lowered 7th

C7sus4 = dominant 7th with the 4th taking the place of the 3rd

C7($\flat$5), C7(-5) = dominant 7th with a lowered 5th

C7($\sharp$5), C7(+5), C7aug, C7aug5 = dominant 7th with a raised 5th

C7($\flat$9), C7(-9) = dominant 7th with a lowered 9th

C7$\sharp$9, C7+9 = dominant 7th with a raised 9th

C9 = dominant 7th with an added 9th

C9sus4 = dominant 9th with the 4th taking the place of the 3rd

C9($\flat$5), C9(-5) = dominant 9th with a lowered 5th

C9($\sharp$5), C9(+5), C9aug, C9aug5 = dominant 9th with a raised 5th

C11 = dominant 9th with added 11th

C13 = dominant 11th with added 13th

C7($\flat$5$\flat$9), C7(-5-9) = dominant 7th with lowered 5th and 9th

C7($\flat$5$\sharp$9), C7(-5+9) = dominant 7th with lowered 5th and raised 9th

C7($\sharp$5$\sharp$9), C7(+5+9) = dominant 7th with raised 5th and 9th

C7($\sharp$5$\flat$9), C7(+5-9) = dominant 7th with raised 5th and lowered 9th

C13($\flat$9), C13(-9) = dominant 13th with a lowered 9th

C13($\sharp$9), C13(+9) = dominant 13th with a raised 9th

---

Cdim7, Co7 = diminished 7th

---

Sus4 = major triad with a 4th substituting for the chordal 3rd

---

C5 = power chord (not really a chord as it consists of only two different notes)

---

Chords divide themselves into three basic groups: major, minor and dominant. Within each of these groups, a range of tension is possible. Major and minor chords are typically the most harmonically stable, while dominant chords have the most tension.

Here are some suggested scales/modes to try over the following chords:

**Major** $\begin{cases} \text{C, Csus2, C6, C6/7, C6/9, Cmaj7, C(add9), Cmaj9 = C major pentatonic,} \\ \text{C major, C Lydian} \\ \text{Cmaj7($\flat$5), Cmaj7($\sharp$11), Cmaj9($\flat$5), Cmaj9($\sharp$11) = C Lydian, C jazz minor (3rd mode)} \end{cases}$

**Minor** $\begin{cases} \text{Cm, Cm6, Cm7, Cm9, Cm6/9, Cm(add9), Cm11, Cm13 = C Dorian, C Aeolian, C} \\ \text{harmonic minor, C jazz minor, C minor pentatonic, C blues} \\ \text{Cm($\sharp$7), Cm($\natural$7) = C harmonic minor, C jazz minor} \\ \text{C$^{\o7}$, Cm7($\flat$5) = C Locrian, C diminished (whole-half), C blues} \\ \text{Cm7($\sharp$5) = C Aeolian, C harmonic minor} \end{cases}$

**Dominant**
$\begin{cases} \end{cases}$

C7, C7sus4, C9, C9sus4, C11, C13 = C Mixolydian, C blues

C7($\flat$5) = C jazz minor (4th mode), C blues

C7($\sharp$5), C7aug, C7aug5, C9($\sharp$5), C9(+5), C9aug5 = C whole-tone, C melodic minor (7th mode)

C7($\flat$9) = C diminished (half-whole), C harmonic minor (5th mode)

C7($\sharp$9) = C blues, C melodic minor (7th mode), C diminished (half-whole)

C7($\sharp$5$\flat$9) = C melodic minor (7th mode)

C7($\sharp$5$\sharp$9) = C melodic minor (7th mode)

C7($\flat$5$\flat$9) = C melodic minor (7th mode), C diminished (half-whole)

C7($\flat$5$\sharp$9) = C melodic minor (7th mode), C diminished (half-whole)

Csus4, C7sus4 = C Mixolydian, C Phrygian, C blues

**Power Chord**
$\begin{cases} \end{cases}$

C5 = C blues, C minor pentatonic, C major, C major pentatonic, C Dorian, C Phrygian, C Lydian, C Mixolydian, C Aeolian, C harmonic minor, C jazz minor

**Diminished**
$\begin{cases} \end{cases}$

C°7 = C diminished (whole-half)

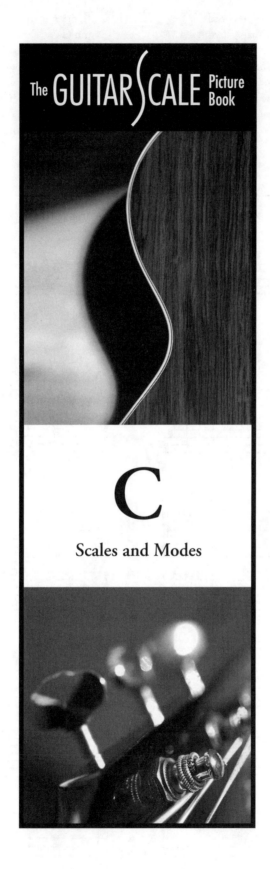

The GUITAR SCALE Picture Book

# C

## Scales and Modes

# C Major

**SCALE DEGREES:** 1 2 3 4 5 6 7
**SCALE TONES:** C D E F G A B

The C major scale (also known as Ionian) can be effectively played over many different C major chords: Csus2, C6, C6/9, Cmaj7, C(add9) and Cmaj9. If you are going to use it to solo over the simpler C major triad, then you'll want to avoid starting and stopping your solo on the 4th and 7th scale degrees. If you eliminate these two scale degrees from the major scale, you are left with the major pentatonic scale.

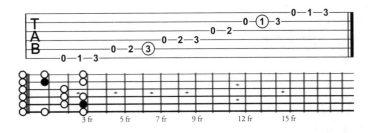

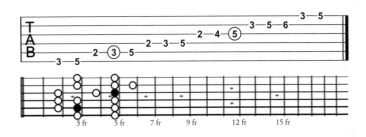

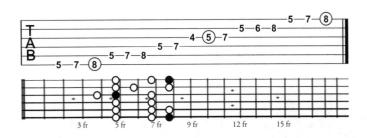

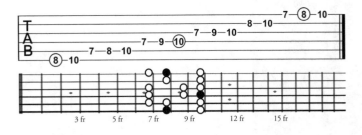

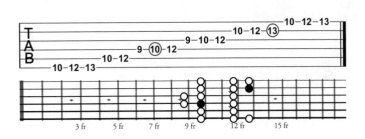

# C Dorian

**SCALE DEGREES:** 1 2 ♭3 4 5 6 ♭7
**SCALE TONES:** C D E♭ F G A B♭

Dorian is the second mode of the major scale. So C Dorian is the same as B♭ major, starting and ending on C.

The Dorian mode is a type of minor scale. It is often used when soloing over minor chords and sounds great when played over these chords: Cm, Cm6, Cm6/9, Cm9, Cm7, Cm(add9), Cm11 and Cm13. It is also possible to play it over a C5 (C power chord). Even though the power chord isn't officially a chord at all, the C Dorian mode will still sound cool over it.

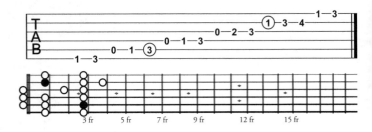

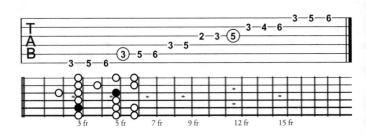

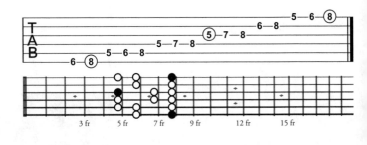

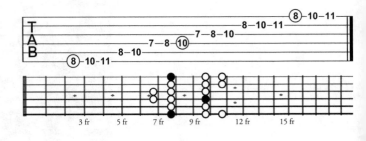

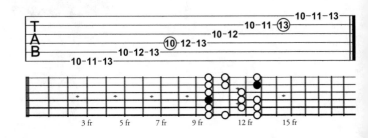

# C Phrygian

**SCALE DEGREES:** 1 ♭2 ♭3 4 5 ♭6 ♭7
**SCALE TONES:** C D♭ E♭ F G A♭ B♭

Phrygian is the third mode of the major scale. So C Phrygian is the same as A♭ major, starting and ending on C.

The sound is very distinctive due to the fact that it begins with a half-step.

Sometimes called a "Spanish" or flamenco scale, its sound is neither clearly major, minor, nor dominant. It is possible to use it over a Cmaj chord, but it is better suited to Csus, C7sus, C7sus(♭9). It also sounds good played over the power chord (C5).

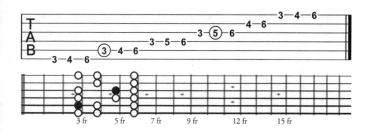

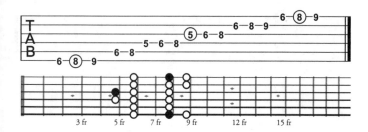

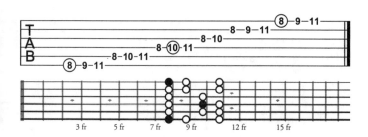

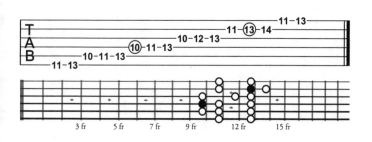

# C Lydian

**SCALE DEGREES:** 1 2 3 ♯4 5 6 7
**SCALE TONES:** C D E F♯ G A B

Lydian is the fourth mode of the major scale. So C Lydian is the same as G major, starting and ending on C.

Lydian is the jazz musician's major scale. The inclusion of the ♯4 imparts an urbane and sophisticated sound. The personality of the scale is found in the 3rd, ♯4th and 7th tones. Focus on these notes when playing this scale.

It will work over these chords: Cmaj, C6, Cmaj7(♭5), Cmaj7(♯11), Cmaj9(♭5), Cmaj9(♯11), C6(♭5), C6/9(♭5), and C6/9(♯11). It will also work over the power chord (C5).

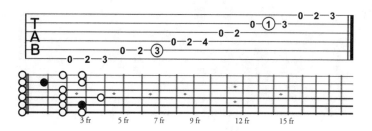

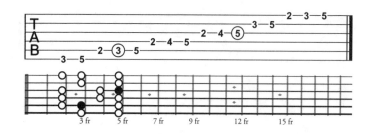

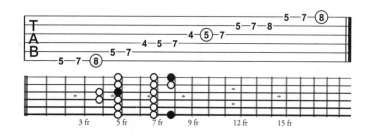

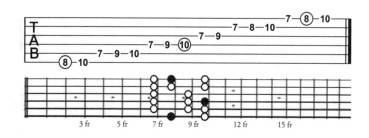

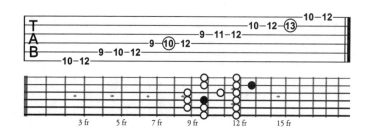

13

# C Mixolydian

**SCALE DEGREES:** 1 2 3 4 5 6 ♭7
**SCALE TONES:** C D E F G A B♭

Mixolydian is the fifth mode of the major scale. So C Mixolydian is the same as F major, starting and ending on C.

The Mixolydian mode is a great blues, soul, R&B, and funk scale. It is often used alongside the blues scale when playing over unaltered dominant chords like: C7, C7sus, C9, C9sus, C11, C13, and C13sus. It will also work over the power chord (C5).

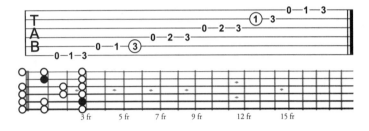

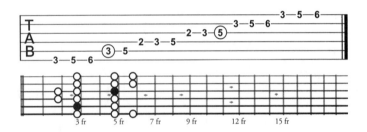

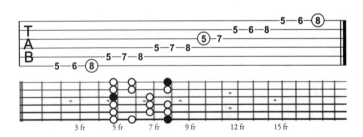

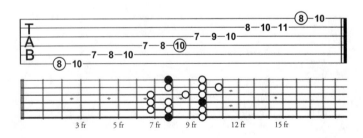

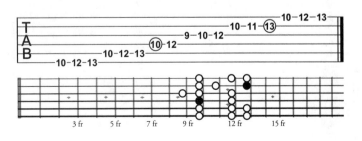

# C Aeolian

**SCALE DEGREES:** 1 2 ♭3 4 5 ♭6 ♭7
**SCALE TONES:** C D E♭ F G A♭ B♭

Aeolian is the sixth mode of the major scale. So C Aeolian is the same as E♭ major, starting and ending on C.

The Aeolian mode is known by several other names: pure minor, natural minor, and relative minor. With so many names you might think this is an important mode, and you'd be correct. This is the mode to use when improvising in minor key songs. It isn't the only scale choice for minor chords (see Dorian, harmonic minor, minor pentatonic and melodic/jazz minor).

In addition to the power chord (C5), this mode will work over Cm, Cm(add9), Cm7, Cm7(♯5), Cm9, and Cm(♯5).

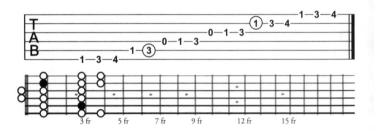

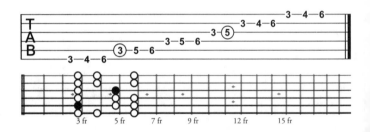

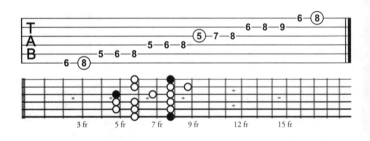

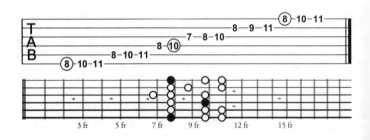

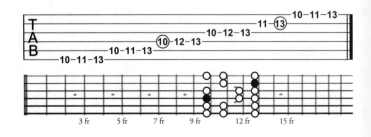

# C Locrian

**SCALE DEGREES:** 1 ♭2 ♭3 4 ♭5 ♭6 ♭7
**SCALE TONES:** C D♭ E♭ F G♭ A♭ B♭

Locrian is the seventh mode of the major scale. So C Locrian is the same as D♭ major, starting and ending on C.

The Locrian mode is the last mode derived from the major scale. It is seldom used in contemporary pop and rock music. Jazz musicians use it when playing over min7(♭5) chords. It has many altered tones, and as such, is unsuitable for use over most other types of minor chords. Use it over Cm7(♭5).

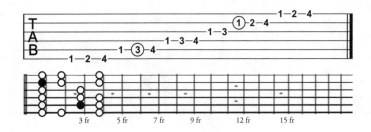

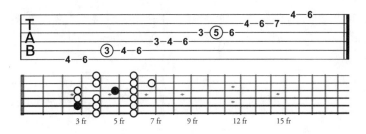

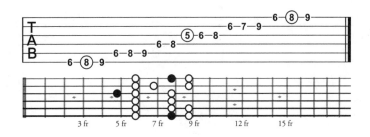

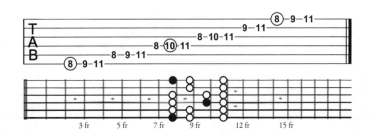

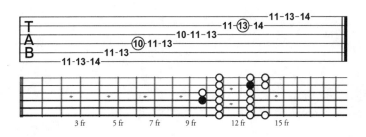

# C Harmonic Minor

C

**SCALE DEGREES:** 1 2 ♭3 4 5 ♭6 7
**SCALE TONES:** C D E♭ F G A♭ B

In construction, this scale is very similar to the Aeolian mode. The only difference between the two is the 7th scale degree. The Aeolian has a lowered 7th.

Some people feel that this scale has a Middle Eastern flavor; others sense a Baroque connection. It is a sound adopted by some metal-style guitarists.

Use it over Cm, Cm(♯7), Cm(maj7), Cm(add9), Cm7, Cm9(maj7), and Cm9(♮7). It will also work over the C power chord (C5).

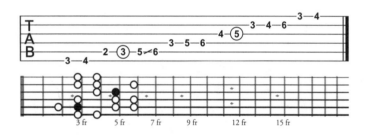

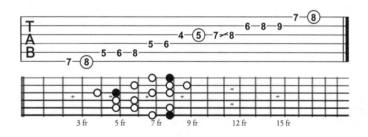

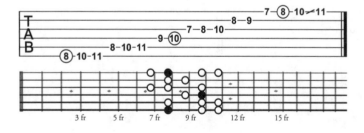

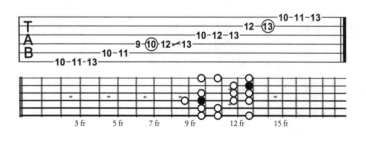

# C Phrygian Dominant

**SCALE DEGREES:** 1 ♭2 3 4 5 ♭6 ♭7
**SCALE TONES:** C D♭ E F G A♭ B♭

Phrygian Dominant is the fifth mode of the harmonic minor scale. So C Phrygian Dominant is the same as F harmonic minor.

It is a scale that is best suited for use when you want to add some tension tones over altered dominant 7th chords. It contains the ♯5 and ♭9 altered tones. These aren't tones you'd typically add to any major or minor chords. It is best suited for C7(♯5), C7(♭9), C13(♭9), and C7(♯5♭9).

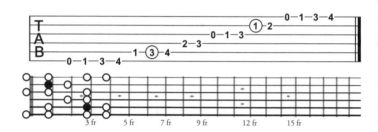

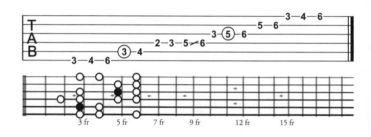

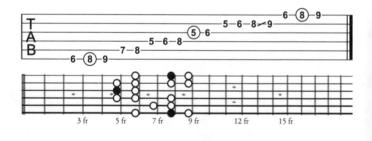

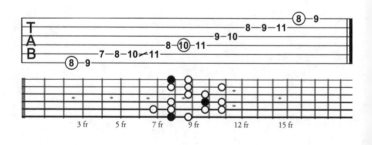

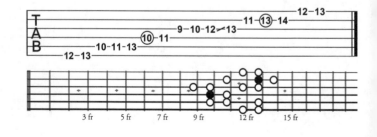

# C Jazz Melodic Minor

**SCALE DEGREES:** 1 2 ♭3 4 5 6 7
**SCALE TONES:** C D E♭ F G A B

There are actually two forms of the melodic minor scale, an ascending form (same as the scale shown here) and a descending form (same notes as the Aeolian mode). For purposes of improvisation, only the ascending version of the scale is used. The term "jazz minor" is used to describe this ascending only version of the scale.

While it is possible to use it over a power chord (C5), this scale is most often played over: Cm, Cm(add9), Cm6, Cm6/9, Cm(♯7), Cm(maj7), Cm(add9), Cm6/9(♯7), and Cm6/9(maj7).

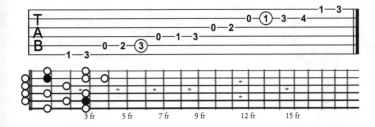

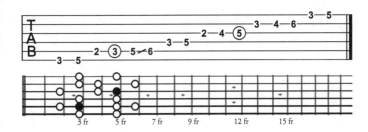

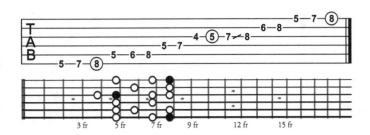

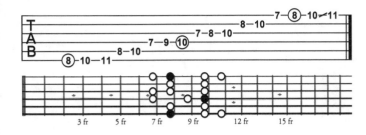

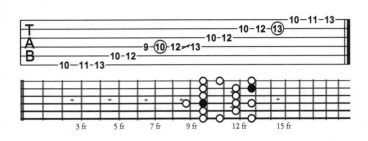

# C Lydian Dominant

**SCALE DEGREES:** 1 2 3 ♯4 5 6 ♭7
**SCALE TONES:** C D E F♯ G A B♭

Lydian Dominant is the fourth mode of the melodic minor scale. So C Lydian Dominant is the same as G melodic minor played from C to C.

Like some of the other scales, this mode goes by a couple of other names: Mixolydian ♯4 and Lydian ♭7. It isn't used as a minor scale by improvisers since it is better suited to dominant chords that contain a ♭5 or ♯11. It is very similar to both the Lydian and Mixolydian modes as the alternate names suggest.

While it is possible to use it over a power chord (C5), this scale is most often played over: C7, C7(♭5), C7(♯11), C9, C9(♭5), C9(♯11), C13(♯11), and C13(♭5).

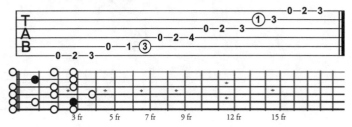

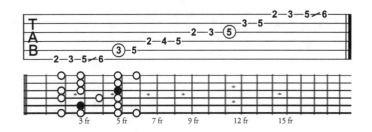

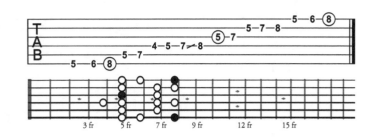

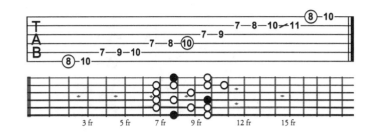

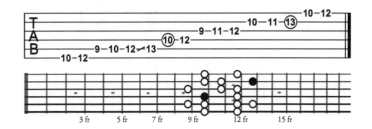

# C Super Locrian

**SCALE DEGREES:** 1 ♭2 ♭3 ♭4 ♭5 ♭6 ♭7
**SCALE TONES:** C D♭ E♭ F♭ G♭ A♭ B♭

Super Locrian is the seventh mode of the melodic minor scale. So C Super Locrian is the same as D♭ melodic minor played from C to C.

The "diminished/whole-tone scale," and "altered scale" are two alternate names for this mode.

This mode contains all of the tension tones that can be absorbed in a dominant chord. These tones are the ♭5, ♯5, ♭9, and ♯9.

Use it over C7, C7(♭5), C7(♯5), C7(♭5♭9), C7(♭5♯9), C7(♯11), C7(♭9), C7(♯9), C13(♭9), and C13(♯9).

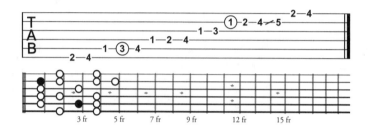

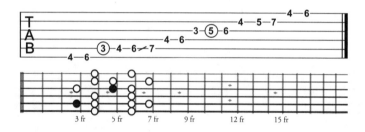

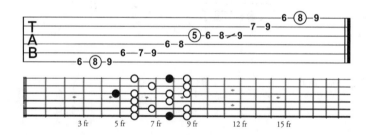

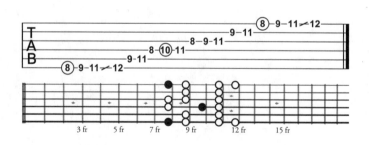

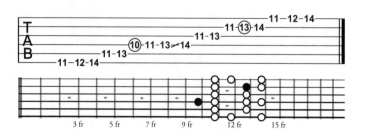

# C Diminished (whole-half)

SCALE DEGREES: 1 2 ♭3 4 ♭5 ♯5 6 7
SCALE TONES: C D E♭ F G♭ G♯ A B

Sometimes called the symmetrical or fully diminished scale, this eight-note scale has some unusual traits. It is useful to understand how the scale is constructed. The primary notes of the scale are those that make up the diminished 7th chord: 1-♭3-♭5-♭♭7. The intervals that occur between these notes are all minor 3rds. The other four notes in this scale are located one half-step below each of these chord tones.

The symmetry in this scale lies in the basic building block of a whole-step followed by a half-step. This "cell" is repeated until the octave is reached.

This symmetry results in the fact that every third note can be considered the root note of the scale. The scale shown here will work with the Cdim7, E♭dim7, G♭dim7, and Adim7 chords. The grey notes in the scale patterns represent these alternate root tones. The scale can be started or ended on either the solid black notes or the grey notes.

Note that the scale pattern repeats itself every three frets, making it quite easy to play at any location on the fingerboard.

# C Diminished (half-whole)

SCALE DEGREES: 1 ♭2 ♭3 ♮3 ♯4 5 6 ♭7
SCALE TONES: C D♭ E♭ E F♯ G A B♭

Like the diminished scale (whole-half), this scale is symmetrical. It is the only mode possible in the diminished scale and it is exactly the same as the whole-half diminished scale, except it begins with a half-step instead of a whole-step. The basic building block consists of a half-step followed by a whole-step. This sequence repeats until the octave is reached.

All of this symmetry results in the fact that every third note can be considered the root note of the scale. The scale shown here will work with the C7, C7(♭9), C7(♯9), C7(♭5), C7(♯11), C13(♭9), C7(♭5♭9), and C7(♭5♯9) chords. The only altered dominant chords that don't work with this scale are the ones that contain a ♯5.

The diminished scales are the only eight note scales in common use. Most scales have seven different notes.

The grey notes in the scale patterns represent alternate root tones. The scale can be started or ended on either the solid black notes or the grey notes.

Note that the scale pattern repeats itself every three frets, making it quite easy to play at any location on the fingerboard. Just transpose either of these patterns up or down the fingerboard a distance of three frets.

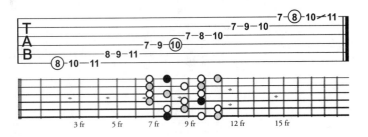

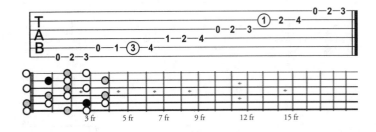

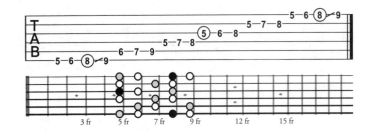

19

# C Major Pentatonic

**SCALE DEGREES:** 1 2 3 5 6
**SCALE TONES:** C D E G A

The major pentatonic scale only has five notes, but it is a scale that is very useful when working in folk, pop, country, and bluegrass styles. This scale avoids the possible dissonance contained in the standard major scale by eliminating the 4th and 7th scale degrees. It can be used over a power chord (C5) as well as Cmaj, C6, C6/9, C(add9), Csus2, Cmaj7 and Cmaj9.

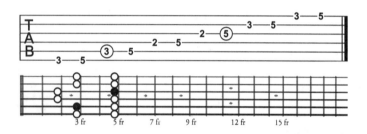

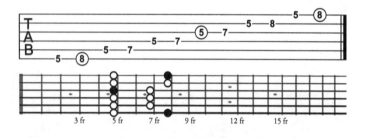

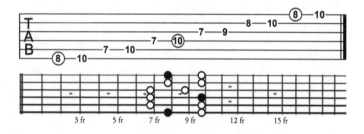

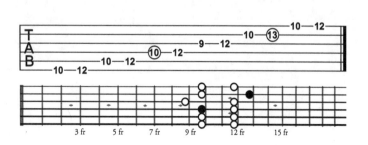

# C Minor Pentatonic

**SCALE DEGREES:** 1 ♭3 4 5 ♭7
**SCALE TONES:** C E♭ F G B♭

Like the major pentatonic, this scale only contains five notes and is often called the rock scale. It can be traced to the Aeolian (natural minor scale) with two notes removed, the 2nd and 6th.

This scale fits over the power chord (C5) as well as over Cm, Cm6, Cm7, Cm6/9, Cm(add9), Cm11, Cm7sus4, Cm13, C7, C9, and C7(♯9). In general, use it when you want a rock sound, even if the chord is major.

Since this scale is very similar to the blues scale, they may be used in place of each other.

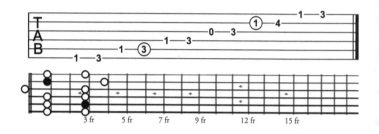

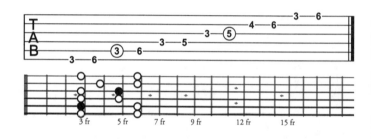

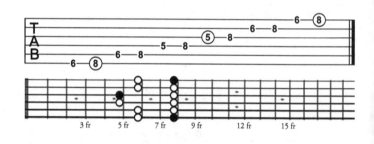

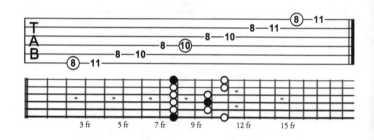

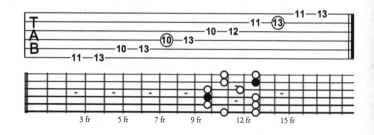

# C Blues

**SCALE DEGREES:** 1 ♭3 4 ♯4 5 ♭7
**SCALE TONES:** C E♭ F F♯ G B♭

This is a six-note scale and is really just a minor pentatonic with the addition of the ♯4.

Use this scale in the same places where you'd use the minor pentatonic, when you want a bluesy/rock effect.

This scale fits over the power chord (C5) as well as over a wide range of other chords in the minor and dominant categories. Try it over: Cm, Cm6, Cm7, Cm6/9, Cm(add9), Cm11, Cm7sus4, Cm13, C7, C9, and C7(♯9). It is even played over some major chords. Try it!

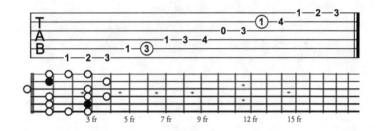

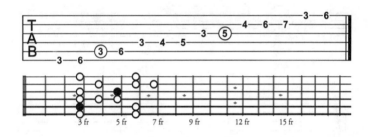

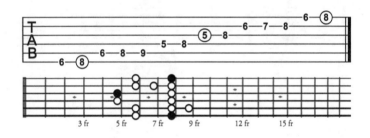

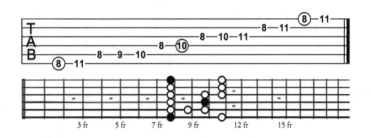

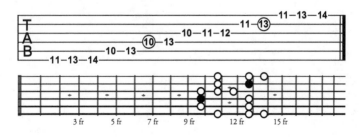

# C Whole Tone

**SCALE DEGREES:** 1 2 3 #4 #5 ♭7
**SCALE TONES:** C D E F# G# B♭

This six-note scale is probably the easiest to finger of any in this book. What makes it so simple is the fact that the distance from one note to the next is always the same, a whole-step. Because of this symmetry, any note in the scale can actually be called the root. The black dots in these patterns represent C notes, but feel free to start and end on any of the tones in the scale.

Only two fingerings are needed to play this scale since any fingering can be moved up or down the neck in two-fret increments.

The sound of this scale is unlike any other in this book due to the lack of half-steps. This lack of half-steps makes the scale feel very unsettled and void of a tonic note. The feeling is akin to falling through space.

This scale works great with C7(#5), C9(#5), C7(♭5), C9(♭5), C13(♭5), or C13(#5).

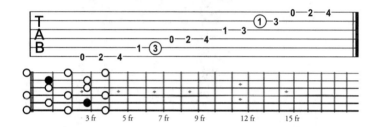

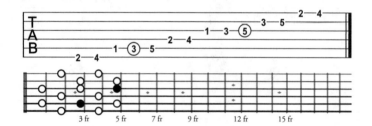

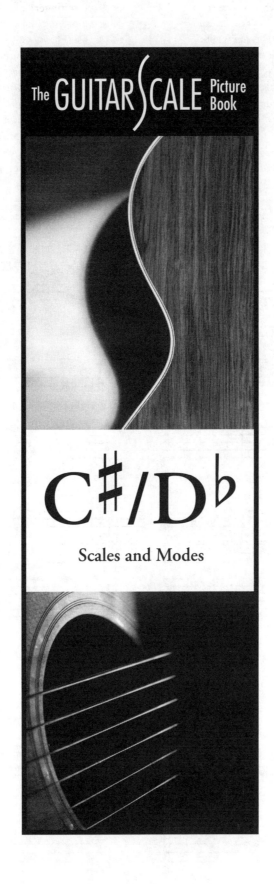

The GUITAR SCALE Picture Book

# C#/Db

## Scales and Modes

# C♯/D♭ Major

**SCALE DEGREES:** 1 2 3 4 5 6 7
**SCALE TONES:** D♭ E♭ F G♭ A♭ B♭ C

The C♯ major scale (also known as Ionian) can be effectively played over many different C♯ major chords: C♯sus2, C♯6, C♯6/9, C♯maj7, C♯(add9) and C♯maj9. If you are going to use it to solo over the simpler C♯ major triad, then you'll want to avoid starting and stopping your solo on the 4th and 7th scale degrees. If you eliminate these two scale degrees from the major scale, you are left with the major pentatonic scale.

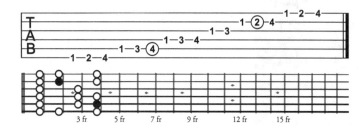

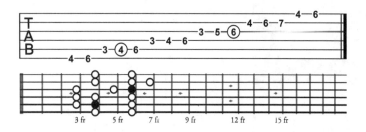

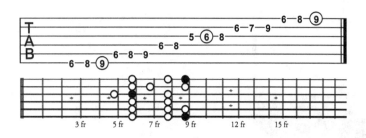

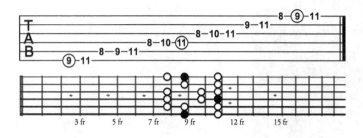

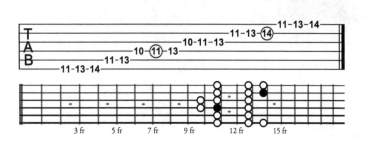

# C♯/D♭ Dorian

**SCALE DEGREES:** 1 2 ♭3 4 5 6 ♭7
**SCALE TONES:** C♯ D♯ E F♯ G♯ A♯ B

Dorian is the second mode of the major scale. So C♯ Dorian is the same as B major, starting and ending on C♯.

The Dorian mode is a type of minor scale. It is often used when soloing over minor chords and sounds great when played over these chords: C♯m, C♯m6, C♯m6/9, C♯m9, C♯m7, C♯m(add9), C♯m11 and C♯m13. It is also possible to play it over a C♯5 (C♯ power chord). Even though the power chord isn't officially a chord at all, the C♯ Dorian mode will still sound cool over it.

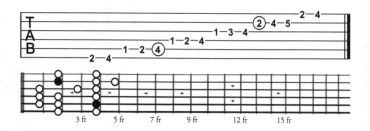

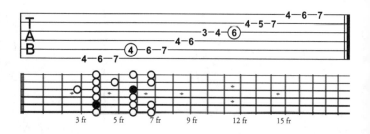

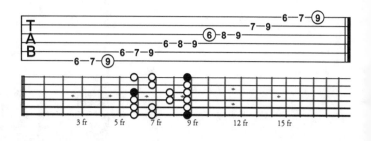

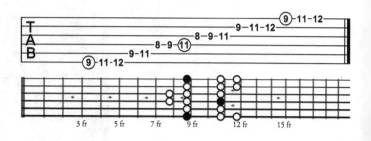

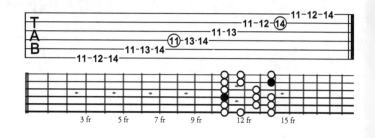

# C♯/D♭ Phrygian

**SCALE DEGREES:** 1 ♭2 ♭3 4 5 ♭6 ♭7
**SCALE TONES:** C♯ D E F♯ G♯ A B

Phrygian is the third mode of the major scale. So C♯ Phrygian is the same as A major, starting and ending on C♯.

The sound is very distinctive due to the fact that it begins with a half-step.

Sometimes called a "Spanish" or flamenco scale, its sound is neither clearly major, minor, nor dominant. It is possible to use it over a C♯maj chord, but it is better suited to C♯sus, C♯7sus, C♯7sus(♭9). It also sounds good played over the power chord (C♯5).

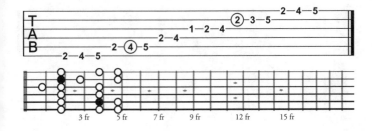

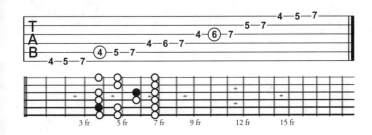

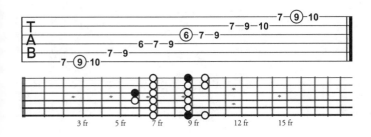

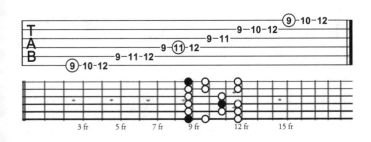

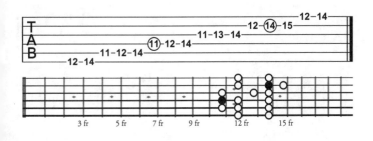

# C♯/D♭ Lydian

**SCALE DEGREES:** 1 2 3 ♯4 5 6 7
**SCALE TONES:** C♯ D♯ E♯ F𝄪 G♯ A♯ B♯

Lydian is the fourth mode of the major scale. So C♯ Lydian is the same as G♯/A♭ major, starting and ending on C♯.

Lydian is the jazz musician's major scale. The inclusion of the ♯4 imparts an urbane and sophisticated sound. The personality of the scale is found in the 3rd, ♯4th and 7th tones. Focus on these notes when playing this scale.

It will work over these chords: C♯maj, C♯6, C♯maj7(♭5), C♯maj7(♯11), C♯maj9(♭5), C♯maj9(♯11), C♯6(♭5), C♯6/9(♭5), and C♯6/9(♯11). It will also work over the power chord (C♯5).

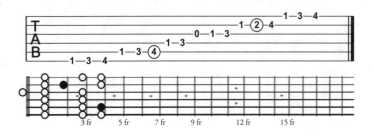

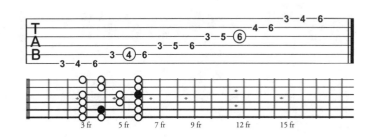

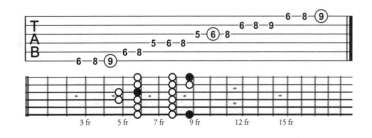

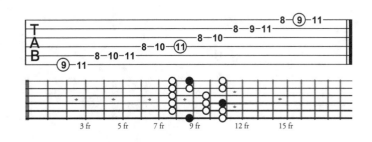

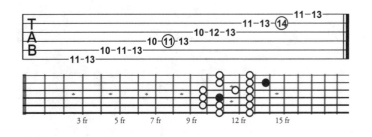

# C#/Db Mixoloydian

**SCALE DEGREES:** 1 2 3 4 5 6 b7
**SCALE TONES:** C# D# E# F# G# A# B

Mixolydian is the fifth mode of the major scale. So C# Mixolydian is the same as F# major, starting and ending on C#.

The Mixolydian mode is a great blues, soul, R&B, and funk scale. It is often used alongside the blues scale when playing over unaltered dominant chords like: C#7, C#7sus, C#9, C#9sus, C#11, C#13, and C#13sus. It will also work over the power chord (C#5).

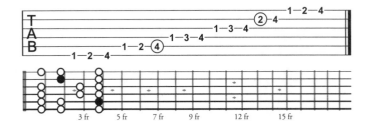

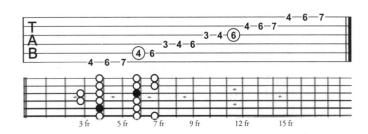

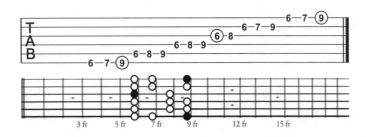

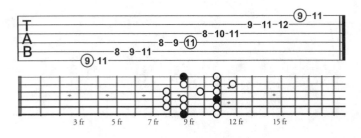

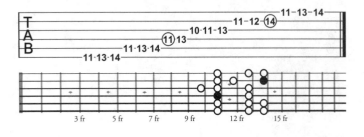

# C#/Db Aeolian

**SCALE DEGREES:** 1 2 b3 4 5 b6 b7
**SCALE TONES:** C# D# E F# G# A B

Aeolian is the sixth mode of the major scale. So C# Aeolian is the same as E major, starting and ending on C#.

The Aeolian mode is known by several other names: pure minor, natural minor, and relative minor. With so many names you might think this is an important mode, and you'd be correct. This is the mode to use when improvising in minor key songs. It isn't the only scale choice for minor chords (see Dorian, harmonic minor, minor pentatonic and melodic/jazz minor).

In addition to the power chord (C#5), this mode will work over C#m, C#m(add9), C#m7, C#m7(#5), C#m9, and C#m(#5).

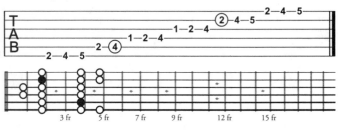

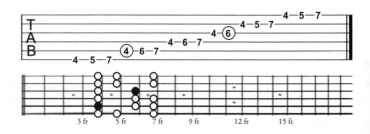

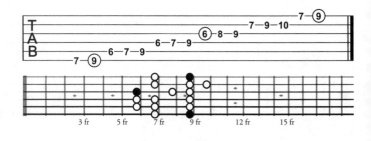

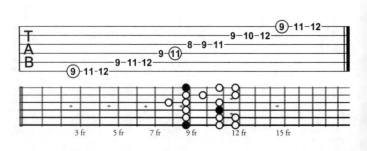

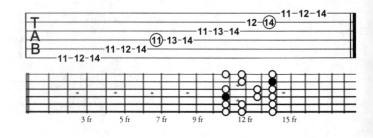

# C♯/D♭ Locrian

**SCALE DEGREES:** 1 ♭2 ♭3 4 ♭5 ♭6 ♭7
**SCALE TONES:** C♯ D E F♯ G A B

Locrian is the seventh mode of the major scale. So C♯ Locrian is the same as D major, starting and ending on C♯.

The Locrian mode is the last mode derived from the major scale. It is seldom used in contemporary pop and rock music. Jazz musicians use it when playing over min7(♭5) chords. It has many altered tones, and as such, is unsuitable for use over most other types of minor chords. Use it over C♯m7(♭5).

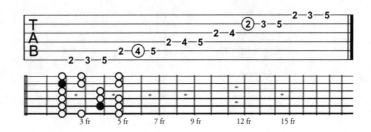

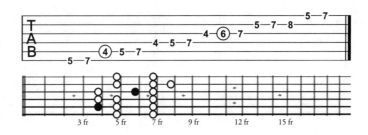

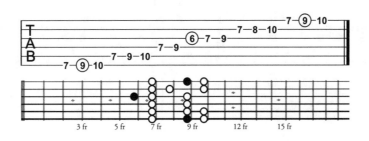

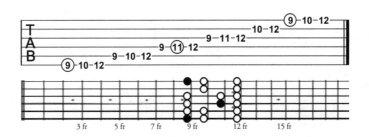

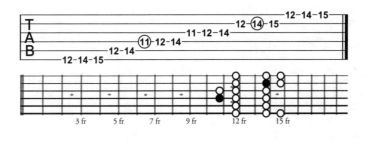

# C#/Db Harmonic Minor

**SCALE DEGREES:** 1  2  b3  4  5  b6  7
**SCALE TONES:** C#  D#  E  F#  G#  A  B#

In construction, this scale is very similar to the Aeolian mode. The only difference between the two is the 7th scale degree. The Aeolian has a lowered 7th.

Some people feel that this scale has a Middle Eastern flavor; others sense a Baroque connection. It is a sound adopted by some metal-style guitarists.

Use it over C#m, C#m(#7), C#m(maj7), C#m(add9), C#m7, C#m9(maj7), and C#m9(b7). It will also work over the C# power chord (C#5).

# C#/Db Phrygian Dominant

**SCALE DEGREES:** 1  b2  3  4  5  b6  b7
**SCALE TONES:** C#  D  E#  F#  G#  A  B

Phrygian Dominant is the fifth mode of the harmonic minor scale. So C# Phrygian Dominant is the same as F# harmonic minor.

It is a scale that is best suited for use when you want to add some tension tones over altered dominant 7th chords. It contains the #5 and b9 altered tones. These aren't tones you'd typically add to any major or minor chords. It is best suited for C#7(#5), C#7(b9), C#13(b9), and C#7(#5b9).

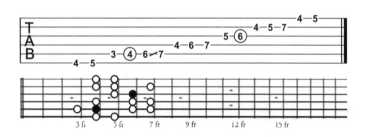

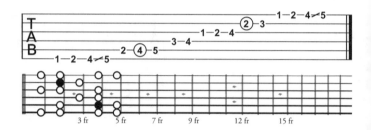

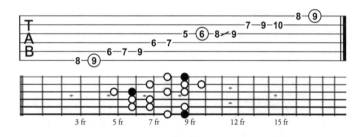

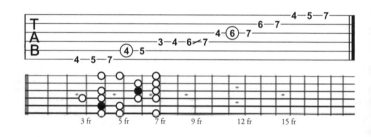

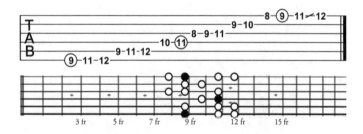

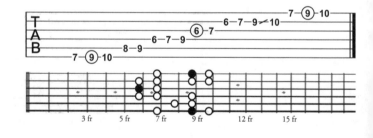

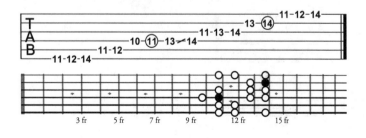

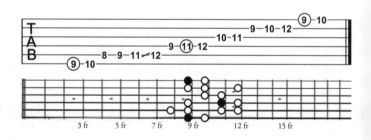

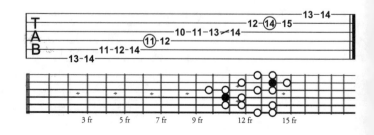

# C#/D♭ Jazz Melodic Minor

**SCALE DEGREES:** 1 2 ♭3 4 5 6 7
**SCALE TONES:** C# D# E F# G# A# B#

There are actually two forms of the melodic minor scale, an ascending form (same as the scale shown here) and a descending form (same notes as the Aeolian mode). For purposes of improvisation, only the ascending version of the scale is used. The term "jazz minor" is used to describe this ascending only version of the scale.

While it is possible to use it over a power chord (C#5), this scale is most often played over: C#m, C#m(add9), C#m6, C#m6/9, C#m(#7), C#m(maj7), C#m(add9), C#m6/9(#7), and C#m6/9(maj7).

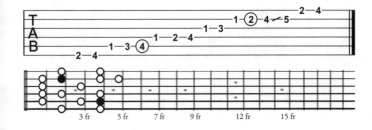

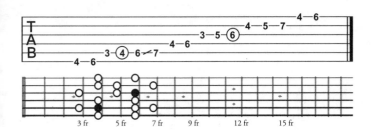

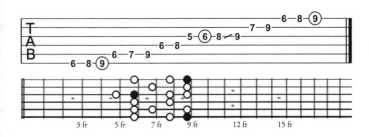

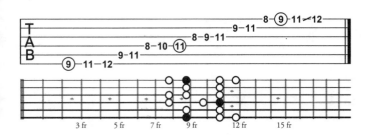

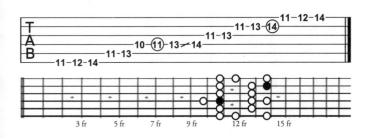

# C#/D♭ Lydian Dominant

**SCALE DEGREES:** 1 2 3 #4 5 6 ♭7
**SCALE TONES:** D♭ E♭ F G A♭ B♭ C♭

Lydian Dominant is the fourth mode of the melodic minor scale. So D♭ Lydian Dominant is the same as A♭ melodic minor played from D♭ to D♭.

Like some of the other scales, this mode goes by a couple of other names: Mixolydian #4 and Lydian ♭7. It isn't used as a minor scale by improvisers since it is better suited to dominant chords that contain a ♭5 or #11. It is very similar to both the Lydian and Mixolydian modes as the alternate names suggest.

While it is possible to use it over a power chord (D♭5), this scale is most often played over: D♭7, D♭7(♭5), D♭7(#11), D♭9, D♭9(♭5), D♭9(#11), D♭13(#11), and D♭13(♭5).

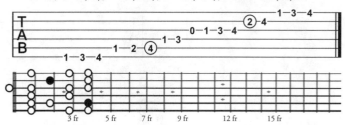

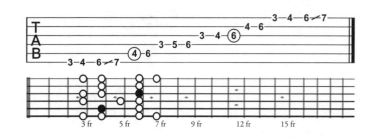

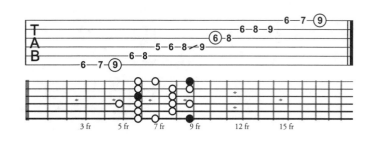

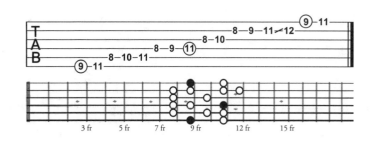

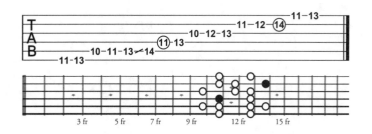

# C#/Db Super Locrian

**SCALE DEGREES:** 1 b2 b3 b4 b5 b6 b7
**SCALE TONES:** C# D E F G A B

Super Locrian is the seventh mode of the melodic minor scale. So C# Super Locrian is the same as D melodic minor played from C# to C#.

The "diminished/whole-tone scale," and "altered scale" are two alternate names for this mode.

This mode contains all of the tension tones that can be absorbed in a dominant chord. These tones are the b5, #5, b9, and #9.

Use it over C#7, C#7(b5), C#7(#5), C#7(b5b9), C#7(b5#9), C#7(#11), C#7(b9), C#7(#9), C#13(b9), and C#13(#9).

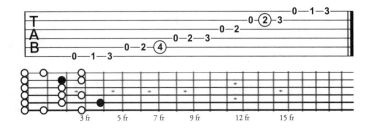

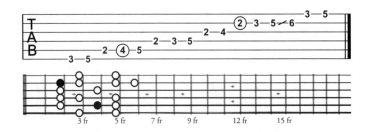

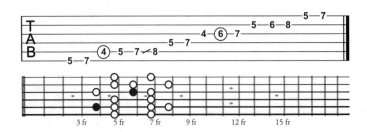

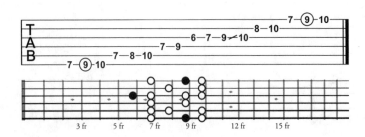

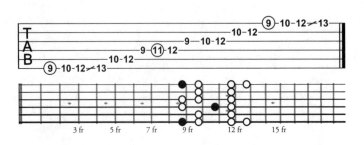

30

# C♯/D♭ Diminished (whole-half)

**SCALE DEGREES:** 1 2 ♭3 4 ♭5 ♯5 6 7
**SCALE TONES:** C♯ D♯ E F♯ G G× A♯ B♯

Sometimes called the symmetrical or fully diminished scale, this eight-note scale has some unusual traits. It is useful to understand how the scale is constructed. The primary notes of the scale are those that make up the diminished 7th chord: 1-♭3-♭5-♭♭7. The intervals that occur between these notes are all minor 3rds. The other four notes in this scale are located one half-step below each of these chord tones.

The symmetry in this scale lies in the basic building block of a whole-step followed by a half-step. This "cell" is repeated until the octave is reached.

This symmetry results in the fact that every third note can be considered the root note of the scale. The scale shown here will work with the C♯dim7, Edim7, Gdim7, and A♯dim7 chords. The grey notes in the scale patterns represent these alternate root tones. The scale can be started or ended on either the solid black notes or the grey notes.

Note that the scale pattern repeats itself every three frets, making it quite easy to play at any location on the fingerboard.

# C♯/D♭ Diminished (half-whole)

**SCALE DEGREES:** 1 ♭2 ♭3 ♮3 ♯4 5 6 ♭7
**SCALE TONES:** C♯ D E F G G♯ A♯ B

Like the diminished scale (whole-half), this scale is symmetrical. It is the only mode possible in the diminished scale and it is exactly the same as the whole-half diminished scale, except it begins with a half-step instead of a whole-step. The basic building block consists of a half-step followed by a whole-step. This sequence repeats until the octave is reached.

All of this symmetry results in the fact that every third note can be considered the root note of the scale. The scale shown here will work with the C♯7, C♯7(♭9), C♯7(♯9), C♯7(♭5), C♯7(♯11), C♯13(♭9), C♯7(♭5♭9), and C♯7(♭5♯9) chords. The only altered dominant chords that don't work with this scale are the ones that contain a ♯5.

The diminished scales are the only eight note scales in common use. Most scales have seven different notes.

The grey notes in the scale patterns represent alternate root tones. The scale can be started or ended on either the solid black notes or the grey notes.

Note that the scale pattern repeats itself every three frets, making it quite easy to play at any location on the fingerboard. Just transpose either of these patterns up or down the fingerboard a distance of three frets.

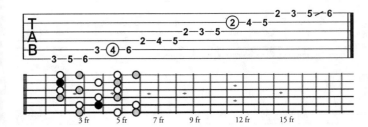

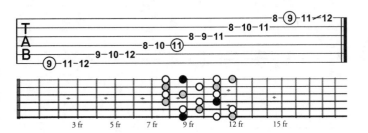

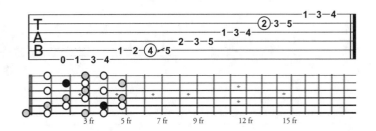

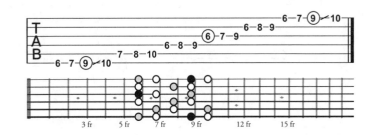

# C#/Db Major Pentatonic

**SCALE DEGREES:** 1 2 3 5 6
**SCALE TONES:** C# D# E# G# A#

The major pentatonic scale only has five notes, but it is a scale that is very useful when working in folk, pop, country, and bluegrass styles. This scale avoids the possible dissonance contained in the standard major scale by eliminating the 4th and 7th scale degrees. It can be used over a power chord (C#5) as well as C#maj, C#6, C#6/9, C#(add9), C#sus2, C#maj7 and C#maj9.

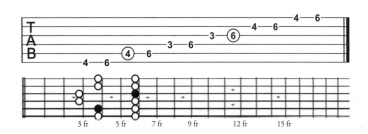

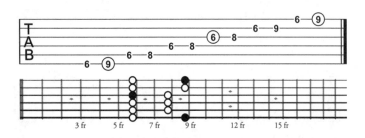

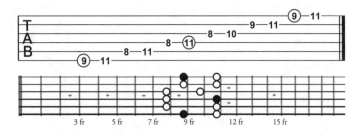

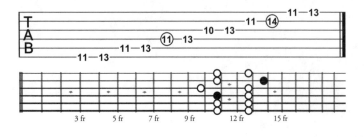

# C#/Db Minor Pentatonic

**SCALE DEGREES:** 1 b3 4 5 b7
**SCALE TONES:** C# E F# G# B

Like the major pentatonic, this scale only contains five notes and is often called the rock scale. It can be traced to the Aeolian (natural minor scale) with two notes removed, the 2nd and 6th.

This scale fits over the power chord (C#5) as well as over C#m, C#m6, C#m7, C#m6/9, C#m(add9), C#m11, C#m7sus4, C#m13, C#7, C#9, and C#7(#9). In general, use it when you want a rock sound, even if the chord is major.

Since this scale is very similar to the blues scale, they may be used in place of each other.

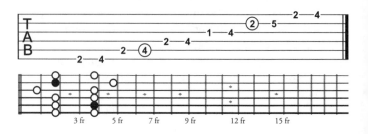

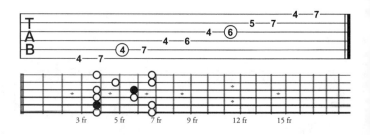

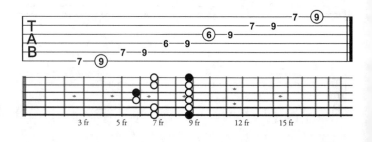

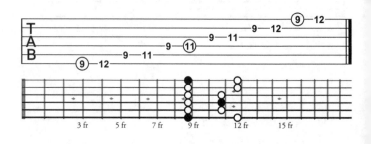

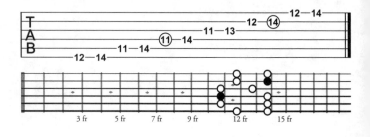

# C#/D♭ Blues

**SCALE DEGREES:** 1 ♭3 4 #4 5 ♭7
**SCALE TONES:** C# E F# F× G# B

This is a six-note scale and is really just a minor pentatonic with the addition of the #4.

Use this scale in the same places where you'd use the minor pentatonic, when you want a bluesy/rock effect.

This scale fits over the power chord (C#5) as well as over a wide range of other chords in the minor and dominant categories. Try it over: C#m, C#m6, C#m7, C#m6/9, C#m(add9), C#m11, C#m7sus4, C#m13, C#7, C#9, and C#7(#9). It is even played over some major chords. Try it!

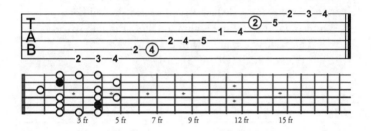

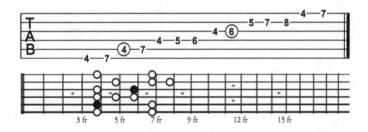

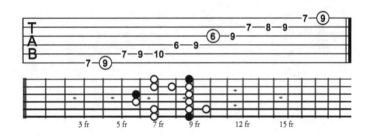

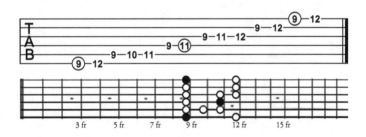

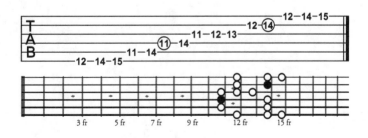

# C#/D♭ Whole Tone

C#
D♭

**SCALE DEGREES:** 1 2 3 #4 #5 ♭7
**SCALE TONES:** D♭ E♭ F G A C♭

This six-note scale is probably the easiest to finger of any in this book. What makes it so simple is the fact that the distance from one note to the next is always the same, a whole-step. Because of this symmetry, any note in the scale can actually be called the root. The black dots in these patterns represent D♭ notes, but feel free to start and end on any of the tones in the scale.

Only two fingerings are needed to play this scale since any fingering can be moved up or down the neck in two-fret increments.

The sound of this scale is unlike any other in this book due to the lack of half-steps. This lack of half-steps makes the scale feel very unsettled and void of a tonic note. The feeling is akin to falling through space.

This scale works great with D♭7(#5), D♭9(#5), D♭7(♭5), D♭9(♭5), D♭13(♭5), or D♭13(#5).

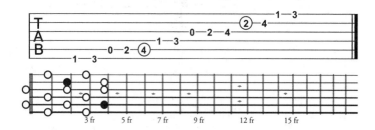

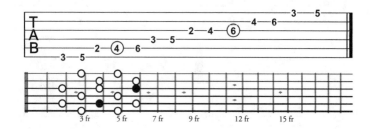

34

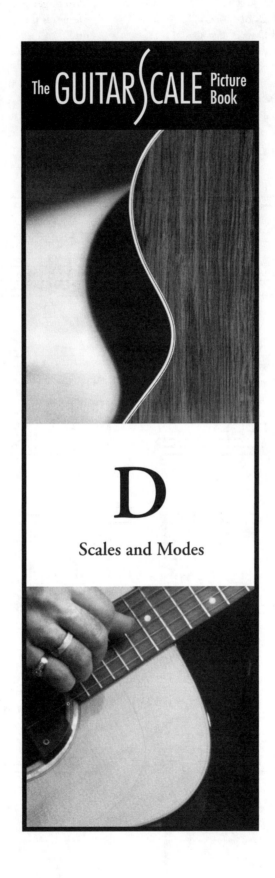

The GUITAR SCALE Picture Book

# D

Scales and Modes

# D Major

**SCALE DEGREES:** 1 2 3 4 5 6 7
**SCALE TONES:** D E F# G A B C#

The D major scale (also known as Ionian) can be effectively played over many different D major chords: Dsus2, D6, D6/9, Dmaj7, D(add9) and Dmaj9. If you are going to use it to solo over the simpler D major triad, then you'll want to avoid starting and stopping your solo on the 4th and 7th scale degrees. If you eliminate these two scale degrees from the major scale, you are left with the major pentatonic scale.

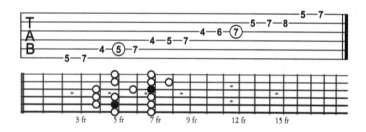

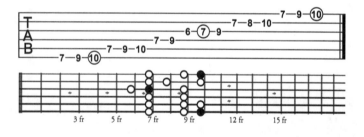

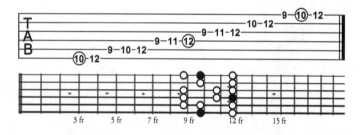

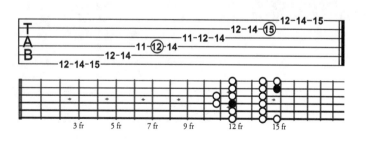

# D Dorian

**SCALE DEGREES:** 1 2 ♭3 4 5 6 ♭7
**SCALE TONES:** D E F G A B C

Dorian is the second mode of the major scale. So D Dorian is the same as C major, starting and ending on D.

The Dorian mode is a type of minor scale. It is often used when soloing over minor chords and sounds great when played over these chords: Dm, Dm6, Dm6/9, Dm9, Dm7, Dm(add9), Dm11 and Dm13. It is also possible to play it over a D5 (D power chord). Even though the power chord isn't officially a chord at all, the D Dorian mode will still sound cool over it.

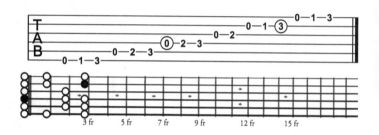

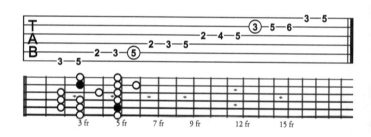

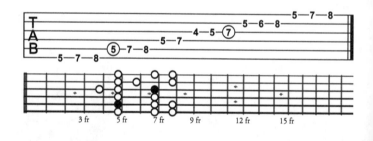

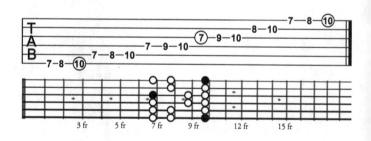

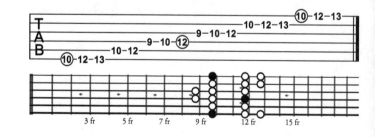

# D Phrygian

SCALE DEGREES: 1 ♭2 ♭3 4 5 ♭6 ♭7
SCALE TONES: D E♭ F G A B♭ C

Phrygian is the third mode of the major scale. So D Phrygian is the same as B♭ major, starting and ending on D.

The sound is very distinctive due to the fact that it begins with a half-step.

Sometimes called a "Spanish" or flamenco scale, its sound is neither clearly major, minor, nor dominant. It is possible to use it over a Dmaj chord, but it is better suited to Dsus, D7sus, D7sus(♭9). It also sounds good played over the power chord (D5).

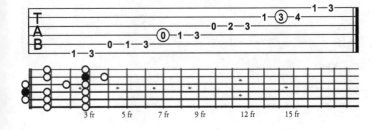

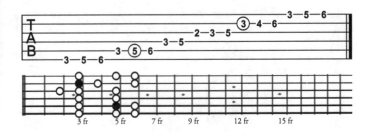

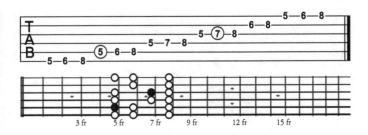

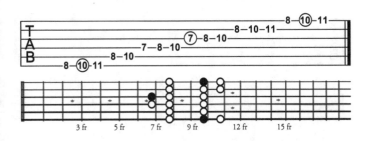

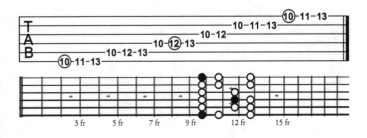

# D Lydian

SCALE DEGREES: 1 2 3 ♯4 5 6 7
SCALE TONES: D E F♯ G♯ A B C♯

Lydian is the fourth mode of the major scale. So D Lydian is the same as A major, starting and ending on D.

Lydian is the jazz musician's major scale. The inclusion of the ♯4 imparts an urbane and sophisticated sound. The personality of the scale is found in the 3rd, ♯4th and 7th tones. Focus on these notes when playing this scale.

It will work over these chords: Dmaj, D6, Dmaj7(♭5), Dmaj7(♯11), Dmaj9(♭5), Dmaj9(♯11), D6(♭5), D6/9(♭5), and D6/9(♯11). It will also work over the power chord (D5).

D

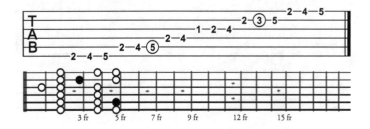

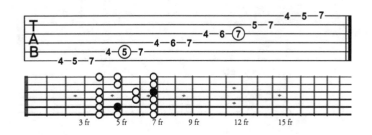

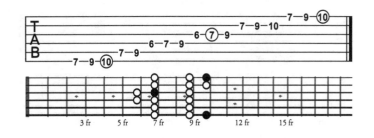

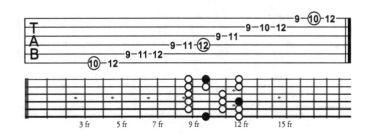

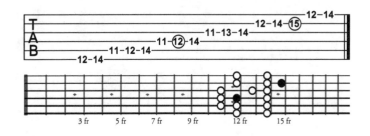

# D Mixoloydian

**SCALE DEGREES:** 1 2 3 4 5 6 ♭7
**SCALE TONES:** D E F♯ G A B C

Mixolydian is the fifth mode of the major scale. So D Mixolydian is the same as G major, starting and ending on D.

The Mixolydian mode is a great blues, soul, R&B, and funk scale. It is often used alongside the blues scale when playing over unaltered dominant chords like: D7, D7sus, D9, D9sus, D11, D13, and D13sus. It will also work over the power chord (D5).

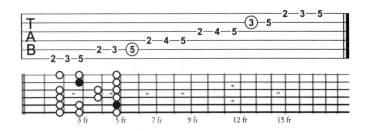

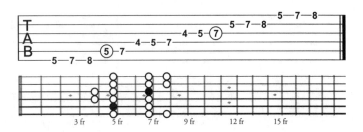

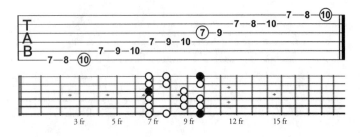

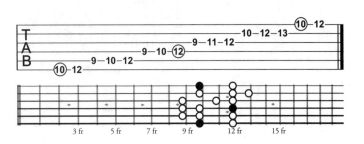

# D Aeolian

**SCALE DEGREES:** 1 2 ♭3 4 5 ♭6 ♭7
**SCALE TONES:** D E F G A B♭ C

Aeolian is the sixth mode of the major scale. So D Aeolian is the same as F major, starting and ending on D.

The Aeolian mode is known by several other names: pure minor, natural minor, and relative minor. With so many names you might think this is an important mode, and you'd be correct. This is the mode to use when improvising in minor key songs. It isn't the only scale choice for minor chords (see Dorian, harmonic minor, minor pentatonic and melodic/jazz minor).

In addition to the power chord (D5), this mode will work over Dm, Dm(add9), Dm7, Dm7(♯5), Dm9, and Dm(♯5).

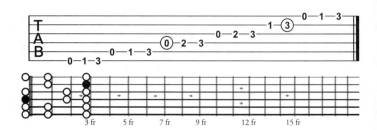

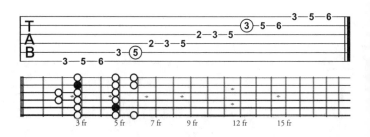

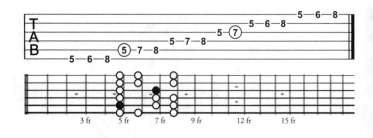

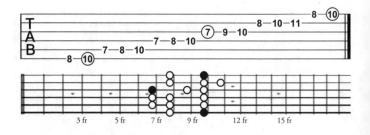

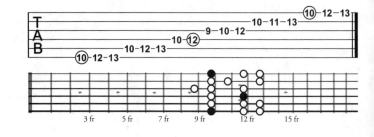

# D Locrian

**SCALE DEGREES:** 1 ♭2 ♭3 4 ♭5 ♭6 ♭7
**SCALE TONES:** D E♭ F G A♭ B♭ C

Locrian is the seventh mode of the major scale. So D Locrian is the same as E♭ major, starting and ending on D.

The Locrian mode is the last mode derived from the major scale. It is seldom used in contemporary pop and rock music. Jazz musicians use it when playing over min7(♭5) chords. It has many altered tones, and as such, is unsuitable for use over most other types of minor chords. Use it over Dm7(♭5).

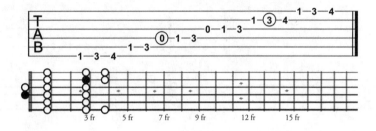

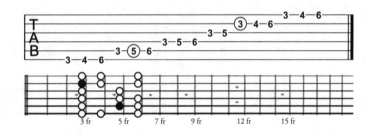

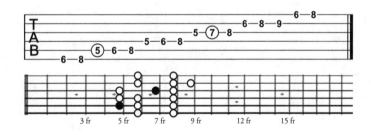

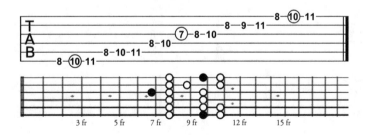

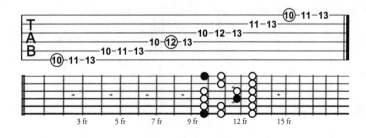

# D Harmonic Minor

**SCALE DEGREES:** 1  2  ♭3  4  5  ♭6  7
**SCALE TONES:**  D  E  F  G  A  B♭  C♯

In construction, this scale is very similar to the Aeolian mode. The only difference between the two is the 7th scale degree. The Aeolian has a lowered 7th.

Some people feel that this scale has a Middle Eastern flavor; others sense a Baroque connection. It is a sound adopted by some metal-style guitarists.

Use it over Dm, Dm(♯7), Dm(maj7), Dm(add9), Dm7, Dm9(maj7), and Dm9(♭7). It will also work over the D power chord (D5).

# D Phrygian Dominant

**SCALE DEGREES:** 1  ♭2  3  4  5  ♭6  ♭7
**SCALE TONES:**  D  E♭  F♯  G  A  B♭  C

Phrygian Dominant is the fifth mode of the harmonic minor scale. So D Phrygian Dominant is the same as G harmonic minor.

It is a scale that is best suited for use when you want to add some tension tones over altered dominant 7th chords. It contains the ♯5 and ♭9 altered tones. These aren't tones you'd typically add to any major or minor chords. It is best suited for D7(♯5), D7(♭9), and D13(♭9), and D7(♯5♭9).

**D**

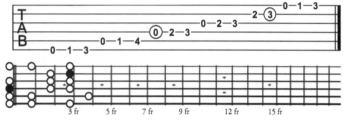

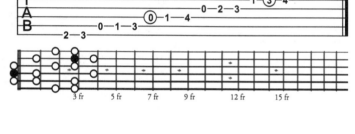

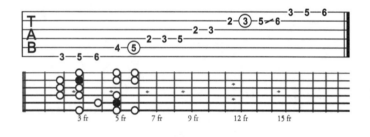

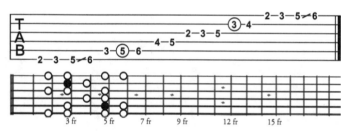

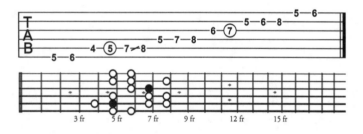

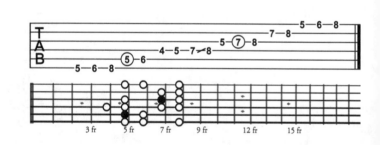

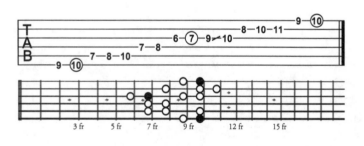

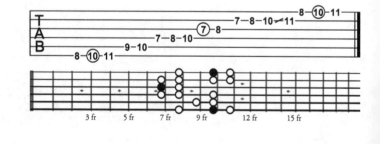

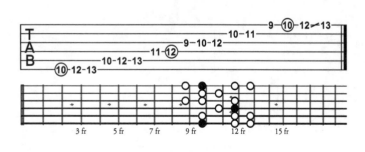

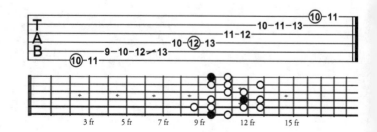

# D Jazz Melodic Minor

**SCALE DEGREES:** 1 2 ♭3 4 5 6 7
**SCALE TONES:** D E F G A B C♯

There are actually two forms of the melodic minor scale, an ascending form (same as the scale shown here) and a descending form (same notes as the Aeolian mode). For purposes of improvisation, only the ascending version of the scale is used. The term "jazz minor" is used to describe this ascending only version of the scale.

While it is possible to use it over a power chord (D5), this scale is most often played over: Dm, Dm(add9), Dm6, Dm6/9, Dm(♯7), Dm(♮7), Dm(add9), Dm6/9(♯7), and Dm6/9(♮7).

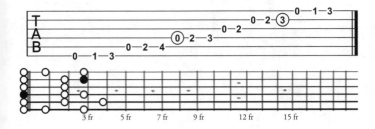

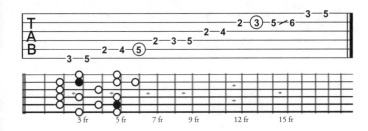

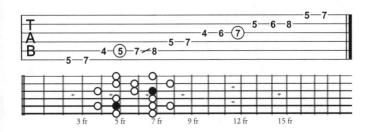

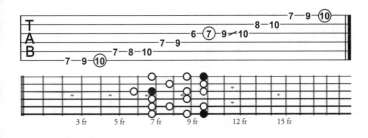

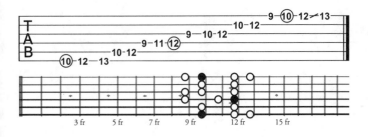

# D Lydian Dominant

**SCALE DEGREES:** 1 2 3 ♯4 5 6 ♭7
**SCALE TONES:** D E F♯ G♯ A B C

Lydian Dominant is the fourth mode of the melodic minor scale. So D Lydian Dominant is the same as A melodic minor played from D to D.

Like some of the other scales, this mode goes by a couple of other names: Mixolydian ♯4 and Lydian ♭7. It isn't used as a minor scale by improvisers since it is better suited to dominant chords that contain a ♭5 or ♯11. It is very similar to both the Lydian and Mixolydian modes as the alternate names suggest.

While it is possible to use it over a power chord (D5), this scale is most often played over: D7, D7(♭5), D7(♯11), D9, D9(♭5), D9(♯11), D13(♯11), and D13(♭5).

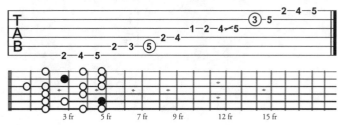

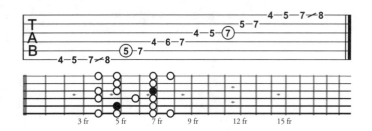

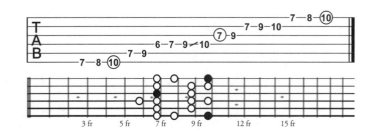

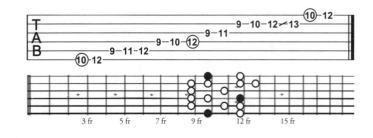

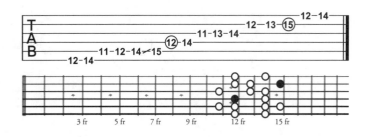

D

# D Super Locrian

**SCALE DEGREES: 1  ♭2  ♭3  ♭4  ♭5  ♭6  ♭7**
**SCALE TONES: D  E♭  F  G♭  A♭  B♭  C**

Super Locrian is the seventh mode of the melodic minor scale. So D Super Locrian is the same as E♭ melodic minor played from D to D.

The "diminished/whole-tone scale," and "altered scale" are two alternate names for this mode.

This mode contains all of the tension tones that can be absorbed in a dominant chord. These tones are the ♭5, ♯5, ♭9, and ♯9.

Use it over D7, D7(♭5), D7(♯5), D7(♭5♭9), D7(♭5♯9), D7(♯11), D7(♭9), D7(♯9), D13(♭9), and D13(♯9).

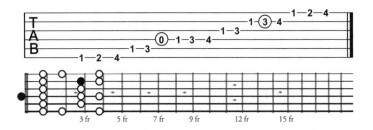

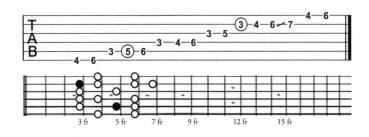

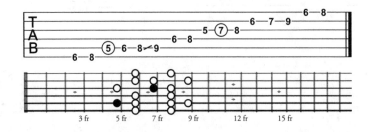

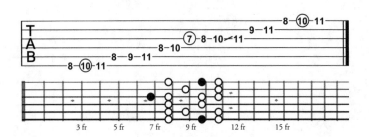

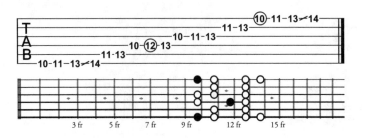

# D Diminished (whole-half)

**SCALE DEGREES:** 1 2 ♭3 4 ♭5 ♯5 6 7
**SCALE TONES:** D E F G A♭ A♯ B C♯

Sometimes called the symmetrical or fully diminished scale, this eight-note scale has some unusual traits. It is useful to understand how the scale is constructed. The primary notes of the scale are those that make up the diminished 7th chord: 1-♭3-♭5-♭♭7. The intervals that occur between these notes are all minor 3rds. The other four notes in this scale are located one half-step below each of these chord tones.

The symmetry in this scale lies in the basic building block of a whole-step followed by a half-step. This "cell" is repeated until the octave is reached.

This symmetry results in the fact that every third note can be considered the root note of the scale. The scale shown here will work with the Ddim7, Fdim7, A♭dim7, and Bdim7 chords. The grey notes in the scale patterns represent these alternate root tones. The scale can be started or ended on either the solid black notes or the grey notes.

Note that the scale pattern repeats itself every three frets, making it quite easy to play at any location on the fingerboard.

# D Diminished (half-whole)

**SCALE DEGREES:** 1 ♭2 ♭3 ♮3 ♯4 5 6 ♭7
**SCALE TONES:** D E♭ F F♯ G♯ A B C

Like the diminished scale (whole-half), this scale is symmetrical. It is the only mode possible in the diminished scale and it is exactly the same as the whole-half diminished scale, except it begins with a half-step instead of a whole-step. The basic building block consists of a half-step followed by a whole-step. This sequence repeats until the octave is reached.

All of this symmetry results in the fact that every third note can be considered the root note of the scale. The scale shown here will work with the D7, D7(♭9), D7(♯9), D7(♭5), D7(♯11), D13(♭9), D7(♭5♭9), and D7(♭5♯9) chords. The only altered dominant chords that don't work with this scale are the ones that contain a ♯5.

The diminished scales are the only eight note scales in common use. Most scales have seven different notes.

The grey notes in the scale patterns represent alternate root tones. The scale can be started or ended on either the solid black notes or the grey notes.

Note that the scale pattern repeats itself every three frets, making it quite easy to play at any location on the fingerboard. Just transpose either of these patterns up or down the fingerboard a distance of three frets.

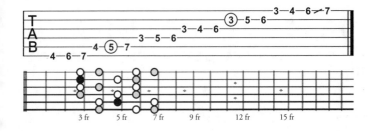

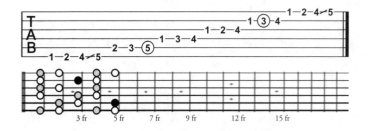

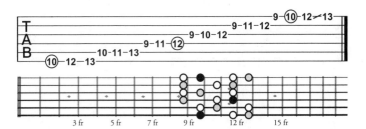

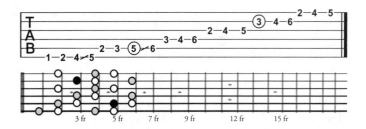

# D Major Pentatonic

**SCALE DEGREES:** 1 2 3 5 6
**SCALE TONES:** D E F# A B

The major pentatonic scale only has five notes, but it is a scale that is very useful when working in folk, pop, country, and bluegrass styles. This scale avoids the possible dissonance contained in the standard major scale by eliminating the 4th and 7th scale degrees. It can be used over a power chord (D5) as well as Dmaj, D6, D6/9, D(add9), Dsus2, Dmaj7 and Dmaj9.

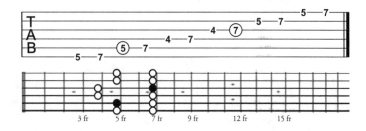

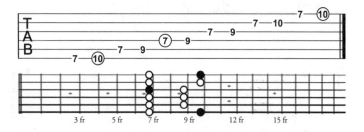

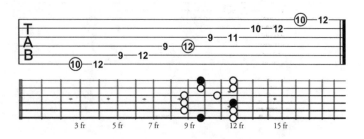

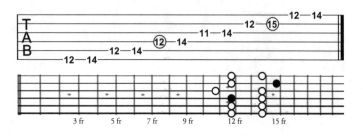

# D Minor Pentatonic

**SCALE DEGREES:** 1 ♭3 4 5 ♭7
**SCALE TONES:** D F G A C

Like the major pentatonic, this scale only contains five notes and is often called the rock scale. It can be traced to the Aeolian (natural minor scale) with two notes removed, the 2nd and 6th.

This scale fits over the power chord (D5) as well as over Dm, Dm6, Dm7, Dm6/9, Dm(add9), Dm11, Dm7sus4, Dm13, D7, D9, and D7(#9). In general, use it when you want a rock sound, even if the chord is major.

Since this scale is very similar to the blues scale, they may be used in place of each other.

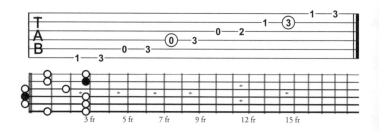

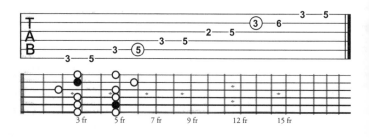

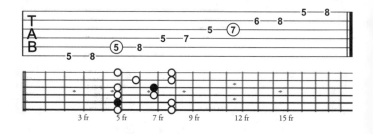

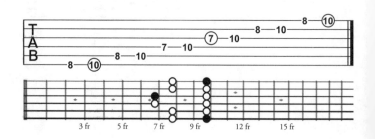

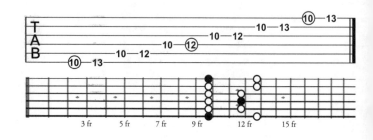

# D Blues

**SCALE DEGREES:** 1 ♭3 4 ♯4 5 ♭7
**SCALE TONES:** D F G G♯ A C

This is a six-note scale and is really just a minor pentatonic with the addition of the ♯4.

Use this scale in the same places where you'd use the minor pentatonic, when you want a bluesy/rock effect.

This scale fits over the power chord (D5) as well as over a wide range of other chords in the minor and dominant categories. Try it over: Dm, Dm6, Dm7, Dm6/9, Dm(add9), Dm11, Dm7sus4, Dm13, D7, D9, and D7(♯9). It is even played over some major chords. Try it!

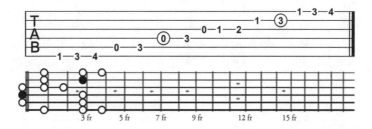

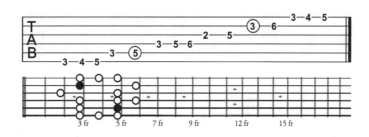

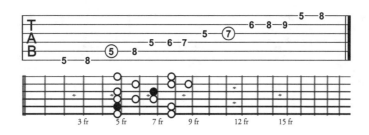

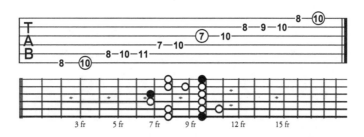

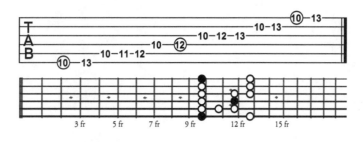

# D Whole Tone

**SCALE DEGREES:** 1  2  3  #4  #5  ♭7
**SCALE TONES:** D  E  F#  G#  A#  C

This six-note scale is probably the easiest to finger of any in this book. What makes it so simple is the fact that the distance from one note to the next is always the same, a whole-step. Because of this symmetry, any note in the scale can actually be called the root. The black dots in these patterns represent D notes, but feel free to start and end on any of the tones in the scale.

Only two fingerings are needed to play this scale since any fingering can be moved up or down the neck in two-fret increments.

The sound of this scale is unlike any other in this book due to the lack of half-steps. This lack of half-steps makes the scale feel very unsettled and void of a tonic note. The feeling is akin to falling through space.

This scale works great with D7(#5), D9(#5), D7(♭5), D9(♭5), D13(♭5), or D13(#5).

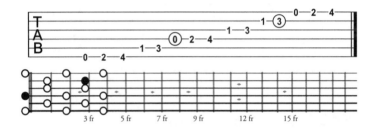

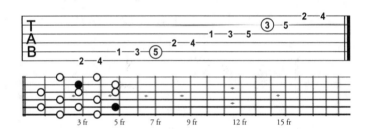

46

The GUITAR SCALE Picture Book

# D#/E♭

### Scales and Modes

# D♯/E♭ Major

SCALE DEGREES: 1 2 3 4 5 6 7
SCALE TONES: E♭ F G A♭ B♭ C D

The E♭ major scale (also known as Ionian) can be effectively played over many different E♭ major chords: E♭sus2, E♭6, E♭6/9, E♭maj7, E♭(add9) and E♭maj9. If you are going to use it to solo over the simpler E♭ major triad, then you'll want to avoid starting and stopping your solo on the 4th and 7th scale degrees. If you eliminate these two scale degrees from the major scale, you are left with the major pentatonic scale.

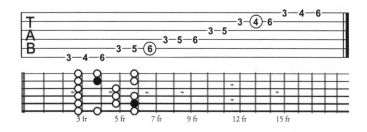

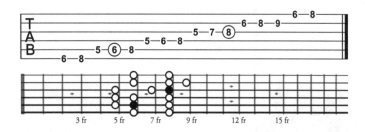

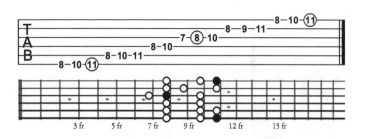

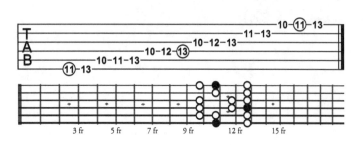

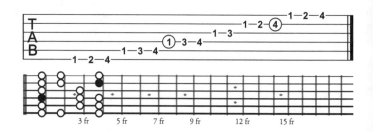

# D♯/E♭ Dorian

SCALE DEGREES: 1 2 ♭3 4 5 6 ♭7
SCALE TONES: E♭ F G♭ A♭ B♭ C D♭

Dorian is the second mode of the major scale. So E♭ Dorian is the same as D♭ major, starting and ending on E♭.

The Dorian mode is a type of minor scale. It is often used when soloing over minor chords and sounds great when played over these chords: E♭m, E♭m6, E♭m6/9, E♭m9, E♭m7, E♭m(add9), E♭m11 and E♭m13. It is also possible to play it over an E♭5 (E♭ power chord). Even though the power chord isn't officially a chord at all, the E♭ Dorian mode will still sound cool over it.

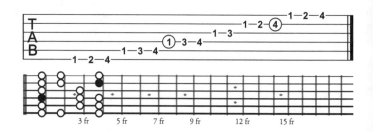

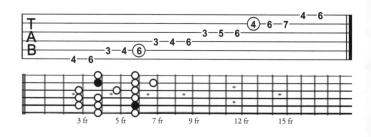

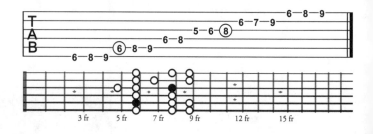

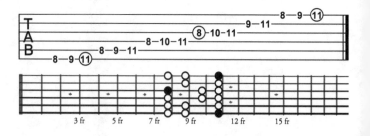

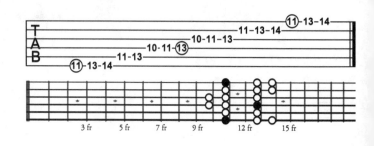

# D#/E♭ Phrygian

**SCALE DEGREES:** 1 ♭2 ♭3 4 5 ♭6 ♭7
**SCALE TONES:** E♭ F♭ G♭ A♭ B♭ C♭ D♭

Phrygian is the third mode of the major scale. So E♭ Phrygian is the same as B major, starting and ending on E♭.

The sound is very distinctive due to the fact that it begins with a half-step.

Sometimes called a "Spanish" or flamenco scale, its sound is neither clearly major, minor, nor dominant. It is possible to use it over a E♭maj chord, but it is better suited to E♭sus, E♭7sus, E♭7sus(♭9). It also sounds good played over the power chord (E♭5).

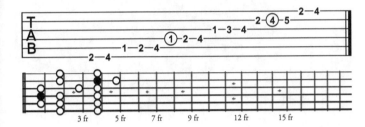

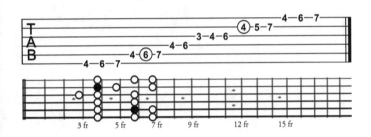

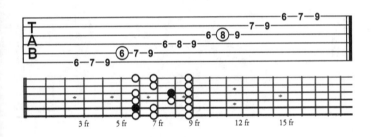

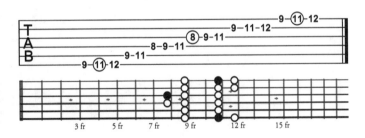

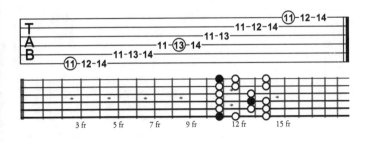

# D#/E♭ Lydian

**SCALE DEGREES:** 1 2 3 #4 5 6 7
**SCALE TONES:** E♭ F G A B♭ C D

Lydian is the fourth mode of the major scale. So E♭ Lydian is the same as B♭ major, starting and ending on E♭.

Lydian is the jazz musician's major scale. The inclusion of the #4 imparts an urbane and sophisticated sound. The personality of the scale is found in the 3rd, #4th and 7th tones. Focus on these notes when playing this scale.

It will work over these chords: E♭maj, E♭6, E♭maj7(♭5), E♭maj7(#11), E♭maj9(♭5), E♭maj9(#11), E♭6(♭5), E♭6/9(♭5), and E♭6/9(#11). It will also work over the power chord (E♭5).

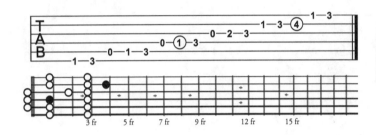

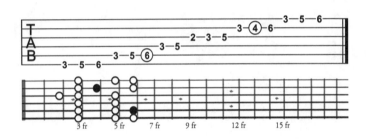

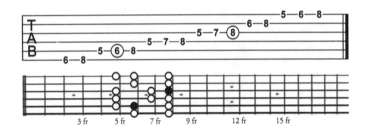

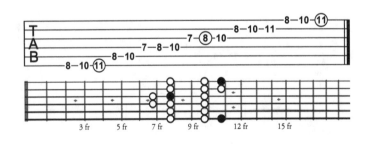

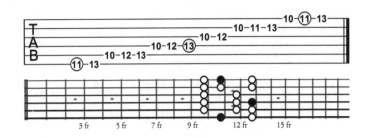

# D♯/E♭ Mixoloydian

**SCALE DEGREES:** 1 2 3 4 5 6 ♭7
**SCALE TONES:** E♭ F G A♭ B♭ C D♭

Mixolydian is the fifth mode of the major scale. So E♭ Mixolydian is the same as A♭ major, starting and ending on E♭.

The Mixolydian mode is a great blues, soul, R&B, and funk scale. It is often used alongside the blues scale when playing over unaltered dominant chords like: E♭7, E♭7sus, E♭9, E♭9sus, E♭11, E♭13, and E♭13sus. It will also work over the power chord (E♭5).

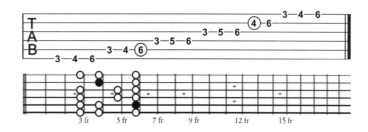

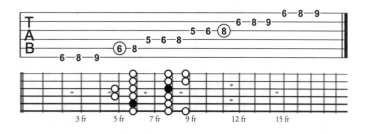

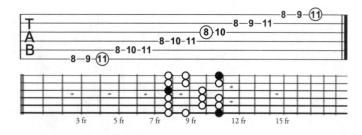

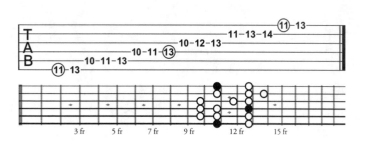

# D♯/E♭ Aeolian

**SCALE DEGREES:** 1 2 ♭3 4 5 ♭6 ♭7
**SCALE TONES:** E♭ F G♭ A♭ B♭ C♭ D♭

Aeolian is the sixth mode of the major scale. So E♭ Aeolian is the same as G♭ major, starting and ending on E♭.

The Aeolian mode is known by several other names: pure minor, natural minor, and relative minor. With so many names you might think this is an important mode, and you'd be correct. This is the mode to use when improvising in minor key songs. It isn't the only scale choice for minor chords (see Dorian, harmonic minor, minor pentatonic and melodic/jazz minor).

In addition to the power chord (E♭5), this mode will work over E♭m, E♭m(add9), E♭m7, E♭m7(♯5), E♭m9, and E♭m(♯5).

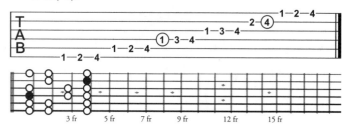

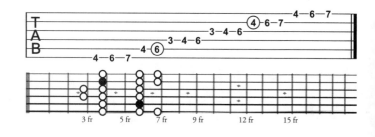

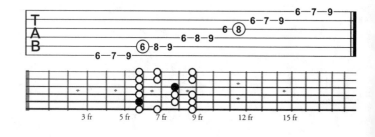

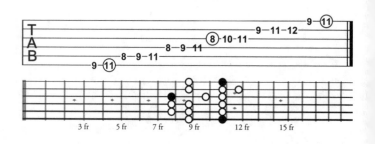

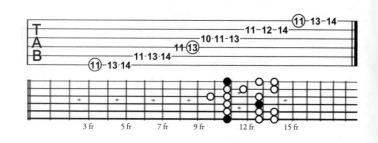

# D♯/E♭ Locrian

**SCALE DEGREES:** 1 ♭2 ♭3 4 ♭5 ♭6 ♭7
**SCALE TONES:** D♯ E F♯ G♯ A B C♯

Locrian is the seventh mode of the major scale. So D♯ Locrian is the same as E major, starting and ending on D♯.

The Locrian mode is the last mode derived from the major scale. It is seldom used in contemporary pop and rock music. Jazz musicians use it when playing over min7(♭5) chords. It has many altered tones, and as such, is unsuitable for use over most other types of minor chords. Use it over D♯m7(♭5).

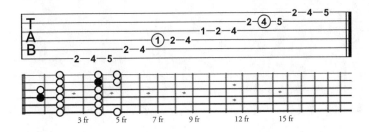

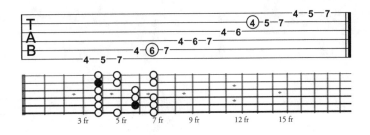

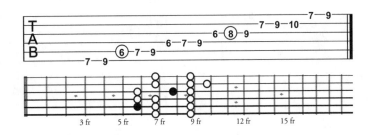

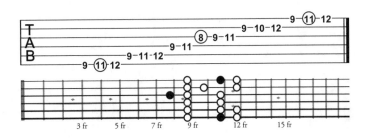

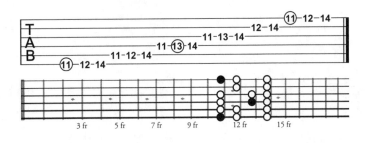

# D#/E♭ Harmonic Minor

**SCALE DEGREES:** 1 2 ♭3 4 5 ♭6 7
**SCALE TONES:** E♭ F G♭ A♭ B♭ C♭ D

In construction, this scale is very similar to the Aeolian mode. The only difference between the two is the 7th scale degree. The Aeolian has a lowered 7th.

Some people feel that this scale has a Middle Eastern flavor; others sense a Baroque connection. It is a sound adopted by some metal style guitarists.

Use it over E♭m, E♭m(#7), E♭m(♮7), E♭m(add9), E♭m7, E♭m9(#7), and E♭m9(♮7). It will also work over the E♭ power chord (E♭5).

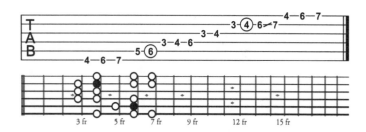

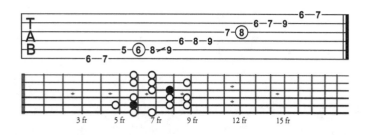

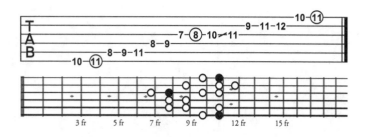

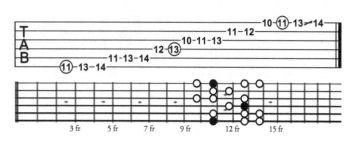

# D#/E♭ Phrygian Dominant

**SCALE DEGREES:** 1 ♭2 3 4 5 ♭6 ♭7
**SCALE TONES:** E♭ F♭ G A♭ B♭ C♭ D♭

Phrygian Dominant is the fifth mode of the harmonic minor scale. So E♭ Phrygian Dominant is the same as A♭ harmonic minor.

It is a scale that is best suited for use when you want to add some tension tones over altered dominant 7th chords. It contains the #5 and ♭9 altered tones. These aren't tones you'd typically add to any major or minor chords. Although it is possible to use it over the power chord (E♭5), it is best suited for E♭7(#5), E♭7(♭9), and E♭13(♭9), and E♭7(#5♭9).

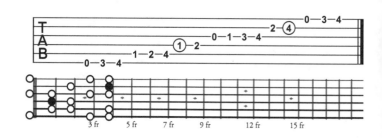

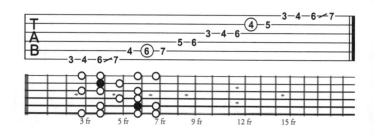

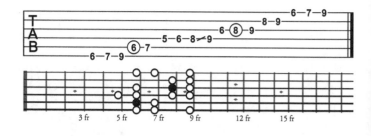

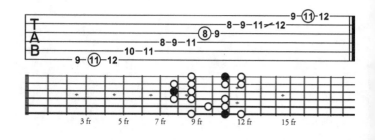

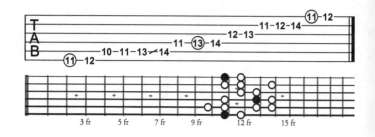

# D#/E♭ Jazz Melodic Minor

**SCALE DEGREES:** 1 2 ♭3 4 5 6 7
**SCALE TONES:** E♭ F G♭ A♭ B♭ C D

There are actually two forms of the melodic minor scale, an ascending form (same as the scale shown here) and a descending form (same notes as the Aeolian mode). For purposes of improvisation, only the ascending version of the scale is used. The term "jazz minor" is used to describe this ascending only version of the scale.

While it is possible to use it over a power chord (E♭5), this scale is most often played over: E♭m, E♭m(add9), E♭m6, E♭m6/9, E♭m(♯7), E♭m(maj7), E♭m(add9), E♭m6/9(♯7), and E♭m6/9(maj7).

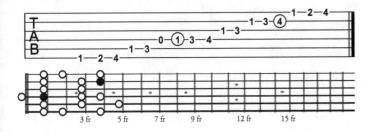

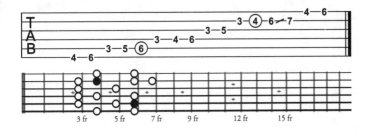

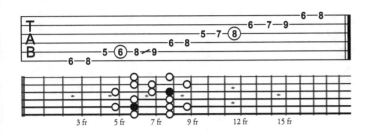

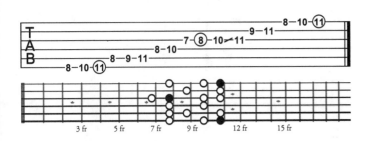

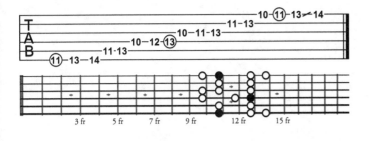

# D#/E♭ Lydian Dominant

**SCALE DEGREES:** 1 2 3 ♯4 5 6 ♭7
**SCALE TONES:** E♭ F G A B♭ C D♭

Lydian Dominant is the fourth mode of the melodic minor scale. So E♭ Lydian Dominant is the same as A♭ melodic minor played from E♭ to E♭.

Like some of the other scales, this mode goes by a couple of other names: Mixolydian ♯4 and Lydian ♭7. It isn't used as a minor scale by improvisers since it is better suited to dominant chords that contain a ♭5 or ♯11. It is very similar to both the Lydian and Mixolydian modes as the alternate names suggest.

While it is possible to use it over a power chord (E♭5), this scale is most often played over: E♭7, E♭7(♭5), E♭7(♯11), E♭9, E♭9(♭5), E♭9(♯11), E♭13(♯11), and E♭13(♭5).

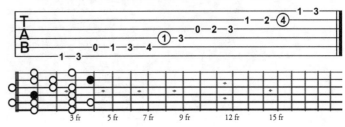

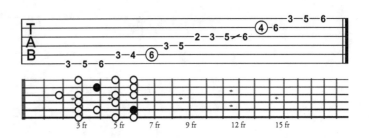

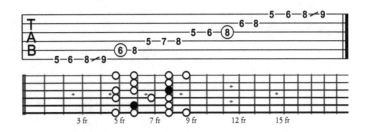

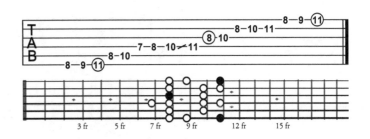

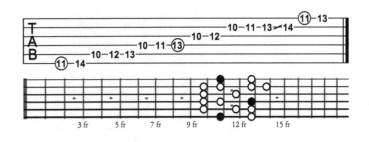

# D♯/E♭ Super Locrian

**SCALE DEGREES:** 1 ♭2 ♭3 ♭4 ♭5 ♭6 ♭7
**SCALE TONES:** D♯ E F♯ G A B C♯

Super Locrian is the seventh mode of the melodic minor scale. So D♯ Super Locrian is the same as E melodic minor played from D♯ to D♯.

The "diminished/whole-tone scale," and "altered scale" are two alternate names for this mode.

This mode contains all of the tension tones that can be absorbed in a dominant chord. These tones are the ♭5, ♯5, ♭9, and ♯9.

Use it over D♯7, D♯7(♭5), D♯7(♯5), D♯7(♭5♭9), D♯7(♭5♯9), D♯7(♯11), D♯7(♭9), D♯7(♯9), D♯13(♭9), and D♯13(♯9).

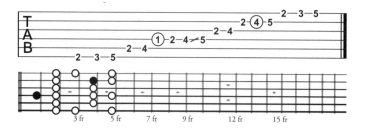

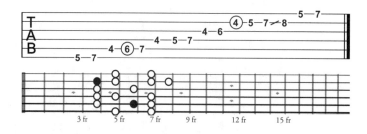

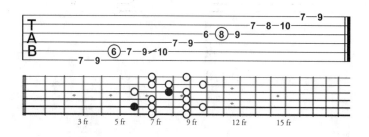

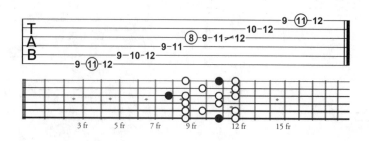

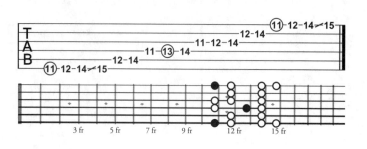

54

# D#/E♭ Diminished, (whole-half)

**SCALE DEGREES:** 1 2 ♭3 4 ♭5 #5 6 7
**SCALE TONES:** E♭ F G♭ A♭ B♭♭ B C D

Sometimes called the symmetrical or fully diminished scale, this eight-note scale has some unusual traits. It is useful to understand how the scale is constructed. The primary notes of the scale are those that make up the diminished 7th chord: 1-♭3-♭5-♭♭7. The intervals that occur between these notes are all minor 3rds. The other four notes in this scale are located one half-step below each of these chord tones.

The symmetry in this scale lies in the basic building block of a whole-step followed by a half-step. This "cell" is repeated until the octave is reached.

This symmetry results in the fact that every third note can be considered the root note of the scale. The scale shown here will work with the E♭dim7, G♭dim7, Adim7, and Cdim7 chords. The grey notes in the scale patterns represent these alternate root tones. The scale can be started or ended on either the solid black notes or the grey notes.

Note that the scale pattern repeats itself every three frets, making it quite easy to play at any location on the fingerboard.

# D#/E♭ Diminished, (half-whole)

**SCALE DEGREES:** 1 ♭2 ♭3 ♮3 #4 5 6 ♭7
**SCALE TONES:** E♭ F♭ G♭ G♮ A B♭ C D♭

Like the diminished scale (whole-half), this scale is symmetrical. It is the only mode possible in the diminished scale and it is exactly the same as the whole-half diminished scale, except it begins with a half-step instead of a whole-step. The basic building block consists of a half-step followed by a whole-step. This sequence repeats until the octave is reached.

All of this symmetry results in the fact that every third note can be considered the root note of the scale. The scale shown here will work with the E♭7, E♭7(♭9), E♭7(#9), E♭7(♭5), E♭7(#11), E♭13(♭9), E♭7(♭5♭9), and E♭7(♭5#9) chords. The only altered dominant chords that don't work with this scale are the ones that contain a #5.

The diminished scales are the only eight note scales in common use. Most scales have seven different notes.

The grey notes in the scale patterns represent alternate root tones. The scale can be started or ended on either the solid black notes or the grey notes.

Note that the scale pattern repeats itself every three frets, making it quite easy to play at any location on the fingerboard. Just transpose either of these patterns up or down the fingerboard a distance of three frets.

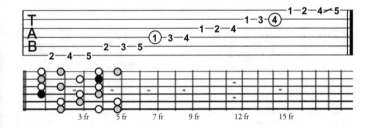

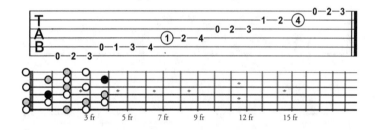

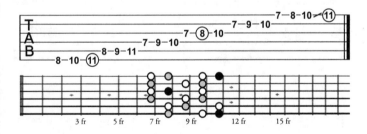

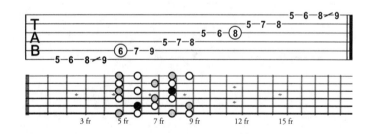

# D#/E♭ Major Pentatonic

**SCALE DEGREES:** 1 2 3 5 6
**SCALE TONES:** E♭ F G B♭ C

The major pentatonic scale only has five notes, but it is a scale that is very useful when working in folk, pop, country, and bluegrass styles. This scale avoids the possible dissonance contained in the standard major scale by eliminating the 4th and 7th scale degrees. It can be used over a power chord (E♭5) as well as E♭maj, E♭6, E♭6/9, E♭(add9), E♭sus2, E♭maj7 and E♭maj9.

D#/E♭

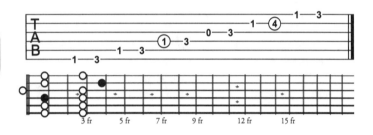

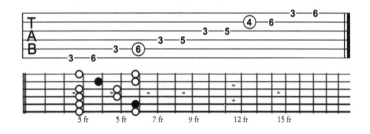

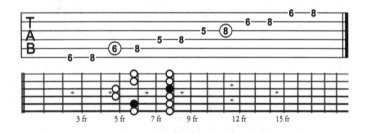

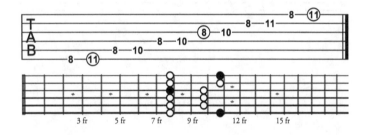

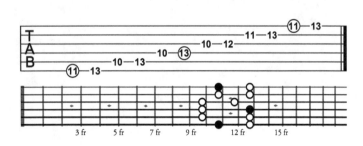

# D#/E♭ Minor Pentatonic

**SCALE DEGREES:** 1 ♭3 4 5 ♭7
**SCALE TONES:** E♭ G♭ A♭ B♭ D♭

Like the major pentatonic, this scale only contains five notes and is often called the rock scale. It can be traced to the Aeolian (natural minor scale) with two notes removed, the 2nd and 6th.

This scale fits over the power chord (E♭5) as well as over E♭m, E♭m6, E♭m7, E♭m6/9, E♭m(add9), E♭m11, E♭m7sus4, E♭m13, E♭7, E♭9, and E♭7(#9). In general, use it when you want a rock sound, even if the chord is major.

Since this scale is very similar to the blues scale, they may be used in place of each other.

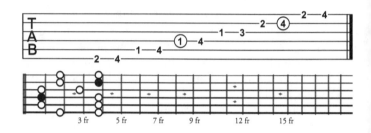

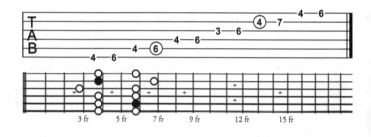

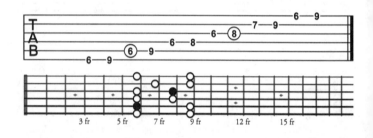

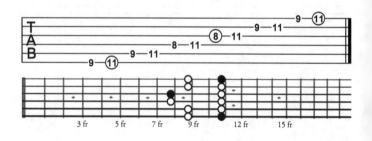

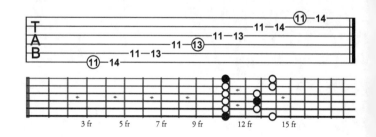

# D♯/E♭ Blues

**SCALE DEGREES:** 1  ♭3  4  ♯4  5  ♭7
**SCALE TONES:** E♭  G♭  A♭  A♮  B♭  D♭

This is a six-note scale and is really just a minor pentatonic with the addition of the ♯4.

Use this scale in the same places where you'd use the minor pentatonic, when you want a bluesy/rock effect.

This scale fits over the power chord (E♭5) as well as over a wide range of other chords in the minor and dominant categories. Try it over: E♭m, E♭m6, E♭m7, E♭m6/9, E♭m(add9), E♭m11, E♭m7sus4, E♭m13, E♭7, E♭9, and E♭7(♯9). It is even played over some major chords. Try it!

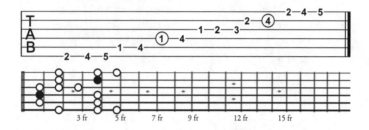

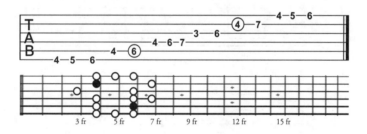

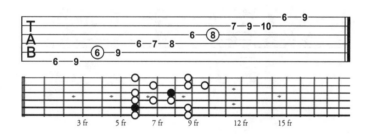

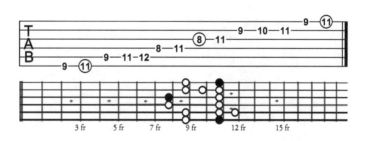

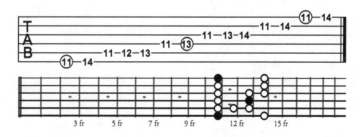

# D♯/E♭ Whole Tone

**SCALE DEGREES:** 1  2  3  ♯4  ♯5  ♭7
**SCALE TONES:** E♭  F  G  A  B  D♭

This six-note scale is probably the easiest to finger of any in this book. What makes it so simple is the fact that the distance from one note to the next is always the same, a whole-step. Because of this symmetry, any note in the scale can actually be called the root. The black dots in these patterns represent E♭ notes, but feel free to start and end on any of the tones in the scale.

Only two fingerings are needed to play this scale since any fingering can be moved up or down the neck in two-fret increments.

The sound of this scale is unlike any other in this book due to the lack of half-steps. This lack of half-steps makes the scale feel very unsettled and void of a tonic note. The feeling is akin to falling through space.

This scale works great with E♭7(♯5), E♭9(♯5), E♭7(♭5), E♭9(♭5), E♭13(♭5), or E♭13(♯5).

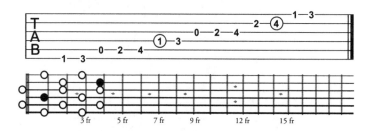

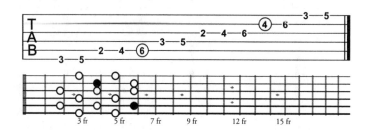

58

The GUITAR SCALE Picture Book

# E

Scales and Modes

# E Major

**SCALE DEGREES:** 1 2 3 4 5 6 7
**SCALE TONES:** E F# G# A B C# D#

The E major scale (also known as Ionian) can be effectively played over many different E major chords: Esus2, E6, E6/9, Emaj7, E(add9) and Emaj9. If you are going to use it to solo over the simpler E major triad, then you'll want to avoid starting and stopping your solo on the 4th and 7th scale degrees. If you eliminate these two scale degrees from the major scale, you are left with the major pentatonic scale.

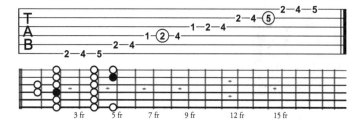

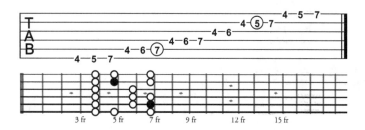

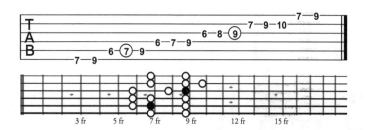

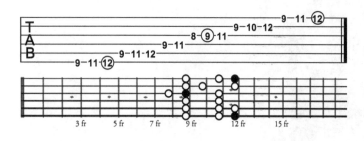

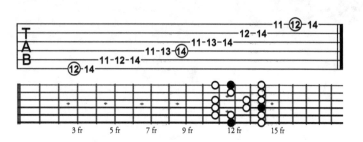

# E Dorian

**SCALE DEGREES:** 1 2 b3 4 5 6 b7
**SCALE TONES:** E F# G A B C# D

Dorian is the second mode of the major scale. So E Dorian is the same as D major, starting and ending on E.

The Dorian mode is a type of minor scale. It is often used when soloing over minor chords and sounds great when played over these chords: Em, Em6, Em6/9, Em9, Em7, Em(add9), Em11 and Em13. It is also possible to play it over a E5 (E power chord). Even though the power chord isn't officially a chord at all, the E Dorian mode will still sound cool over it.

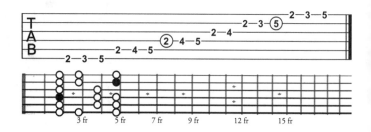

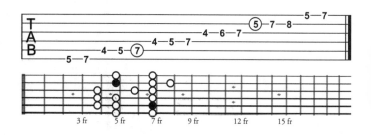

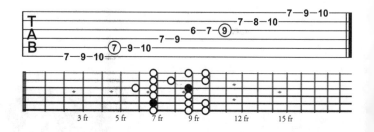

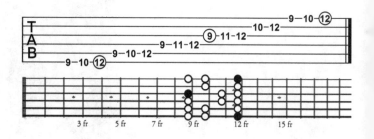

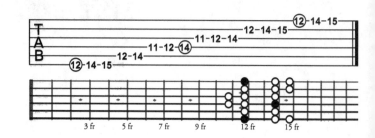

# E Phrygian

**SCALE DEGREES:** 1 ♭2 ♭3 4 5 ♭6 ♭7
**SCALE TONES:** E F G A B C D

Phrygian is the third mode of the major scale. So E Phrygian is the same as C major, starting and ending on E.

The sound is very distinctive due to the fact that it begins with a half-step.

Sometimes called a "Spanish" or flamenco scale, its sound is neither clearly major, minor, nor dominant. It is possible to use it over a Emaj chord, but it is better suited to Esus, E7sus, E7sus(♭9). It also sounds good played over the power chord (E5).

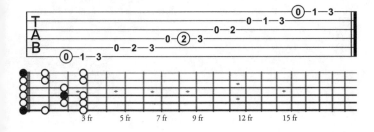

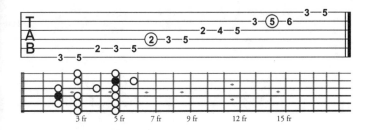

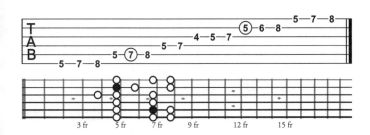

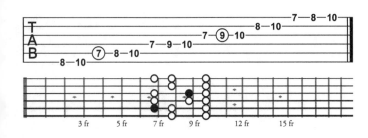

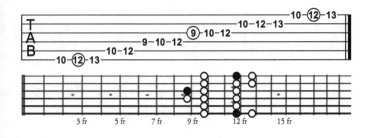

# E Lydian

**SCALE DEGREES:** 1 2 3 ♯4 5 6 7
**SCALE TONES:** E F♯ G♯ A♯ B C♯ D♯

Lydian is the fourth mode of the major scale. So E Lydian is the same as B major, starting and ending on E.

Lydian is the jazz musician's major scale. The inclusion of the ♯4 imparts an urbane and sophisticated sound. The personality of the scale is found in the 3rd, ♯4th and 7th tones. Focus on these notes when playing this scale.

It will work over these chords: Emaj, E6, Emaj7(♭5), Emaj7(♯11), Emaj9(♭5), Emaj9(♯11), E6(♭5), E6/9(♭5), and E6/9(♯11). It will also work over the power chord (E5).

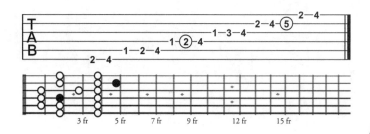

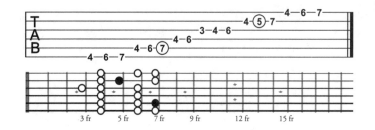

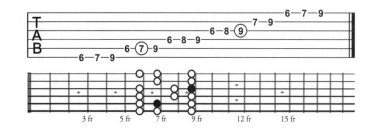

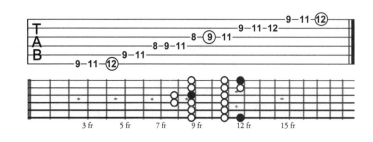

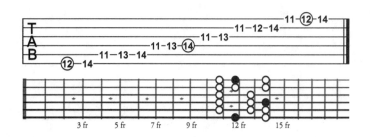

E

61

# E Mixoloydian

**SCALE DEGREES:** 1 2 3 4 5 6 ♭7
**SCALE TONES:** E F♯ G♯ A B C♯ D

Mixolydian is the fifth mode of the major scale. So E Mixolydian is the same as A major, starting and ending on E.

The Mixolydian mode is a great blues, soul, R&B, and funk scale. It is often used alongside the blues scale when playing over unaltered dominant chords like: E7, E7sus, E9, E9sus, E11, E13, and E13sus. It will also work over the power chord (E5).

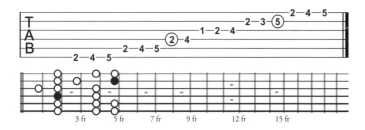

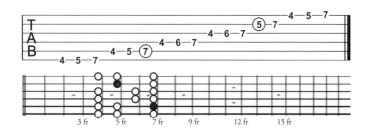

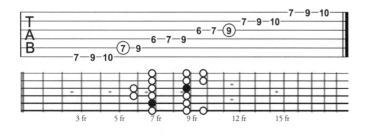

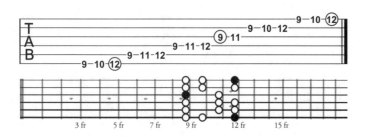

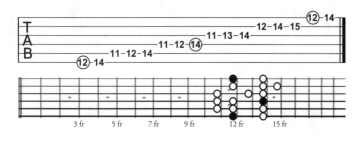

# E Aeolian

**SCALE DEGREES:** 1 2 ♭3 4 5 ♭6 ♭7
**SCALE TONES:** E F♯ G A B C D

Aeolian is the sixth mode of the major scale. So E Aeolian is the same as G major, starting and ending on E.

The Aeolian mode is known by several other names: pure minor, natural minor, and relative minor. With so many names you might think this is an important mode, and you'd be correct. This is the mode to use when improvising in minor key songs. It isn't the only scale choice for minor chords (see Dorian, harmonic minor, minor pentatonic and melodic/jazz minor).

In addition to the power chord (E5), this mode will work over Em, Em(add9), Em7, Em7(♯5), Em9, and Em(♯5).

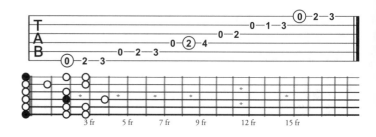

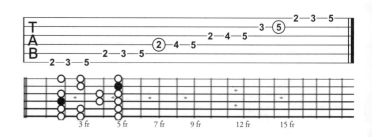

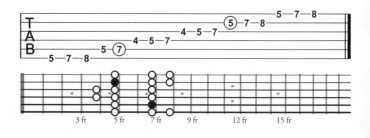

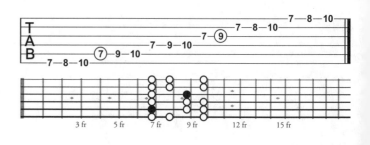

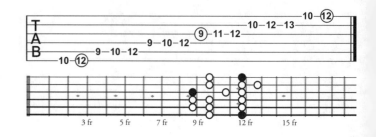

# E Locrian

**SCALE DEGREES:** 1 ♭2 ♭3 4 ♭5 ♭6 ♭7
**SCALE TONES:** E F G A B♭ C D

Locrian is the seventh mode of the major scale. So E Locrian is the same as F major, starting and ending on E.

The Locrian mode is the last mode derived from the major scale. It is seldom used in contemporary pop and rock music. Jazz musicians use it when playing over min7(♭5) chords. It has many altered tones, and as such, is unsuitable for use over most other types of minor chords. Use it over Em7(♭5).

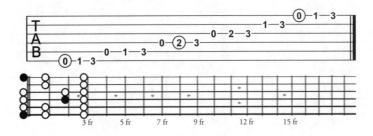

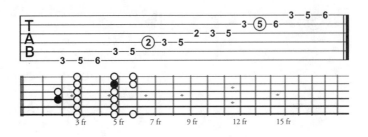

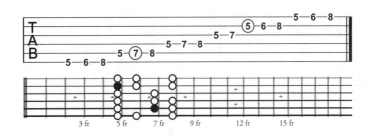

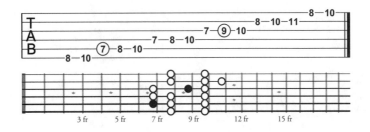

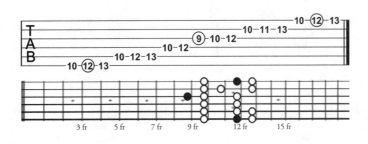

# E Harmonic Minor

**SCALE DEGREES:** 1 2 ♭3 4 5 ♭6 7
**SCALE TONES:** E F♯ G A B C D♯

In construction, this scale is very similar to the Aeolian mode. The only difference between the two is the 7th scale degree. The Aeolian has a lowered 7th.

Some people feel that this scale has a Middle Eastern flavor; others sense a Baroque connection. It is a sound adopted by some metal style guitarists.

Use it over Em, Em(♯7), Em(♮7), Em(add9), Em7, Em9(♯7), and Em9(♮7). It will also work over the E power chord (E5).

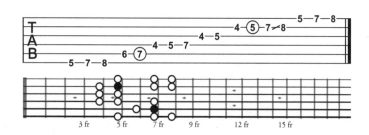

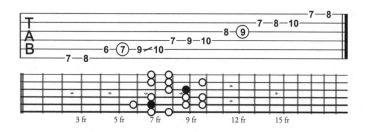

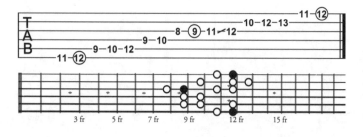

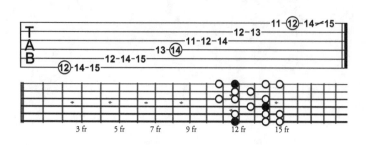

# E Phrygian Dominant

**SCALE DEGREES:** 1 ♭2 3 4 5 ♭6 ♭7
**SCALE TONES:** E F G♯ A B C D

Phrygian Dominant is the fifth mode of the harmonic minor scale. So E Phrygian Dominant is the same as A harmonic minor.

It is a scale that is best suited for use when you want to add some tension tones over altered dominant 7th chords. It contains the ♯5 and ♭9 altered tones. These aren't tones you'd typically add to any major or minor chords. It is best suited for E7(♯5), E7(♭9), E13(♭9), and E7(♯5♭9).

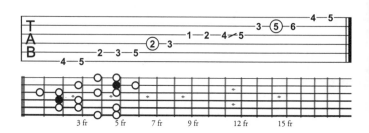

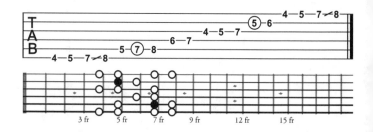

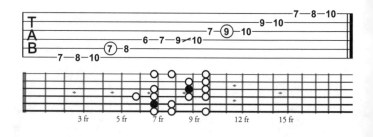

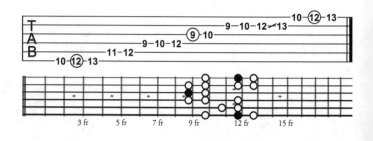

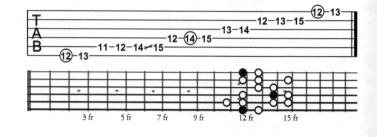

# E Jazz Melodic Minor

SCALE DEGREES: 1 2 ♭3 4 5 6 7
SCALE TONES: E F♯ G A B C♯ D♯

There are actually two forms of the melodic minor scale, an ascending form (same as the scale shown here) and a descending form (same notes as the Aeolian mode). For purposes of improvisation, only the ascending version of the scale is used. The term "jazz minor" is used to describe this ascending only version of the scale.

While it is possible to use it over a power chord (E5), this scale is most often played over: Em, Em(add9), Em6, Em6/9, Em(♯7), Em(maj7), Em(add9), Em6/9(♯7), and Em6/9(maj7).

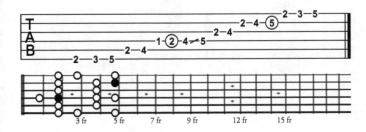

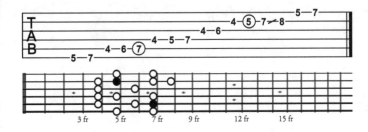

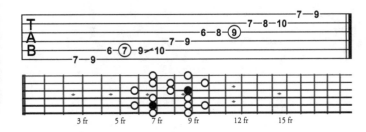

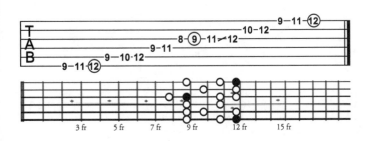

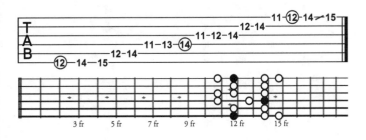

# E Lydian Dominant

SCALE DEGREES: 1 2 3 ♯4 5 6 ♭7
SCALE TONES: E F♯ G♯ A♯ B C♯ D

Lydian Dominant is the fourth mode of the melodic minor scale. So E Lydian Dominant is the same as B melodic minor played from E to E.

Like some of the other scales, this mode goes by a couple of other names: Mixolydian ♯4 and Lydian ♭7. It isn't used as a minor scale by improvisers since it is better suited to dominant chords that contain a ♭5 or ♯11. It is very similar to both the Lydian and Mixolydian modes as the alternate names suggest.

While it is possible to use it over a power chord (E5), this scale is most often played over: E7, E7(♭5), E7(♯11), E9, E9(♭5), E9(♯11), E13(♯11), and E13(♭5).

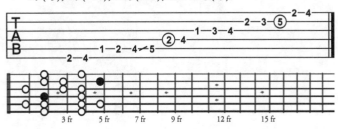

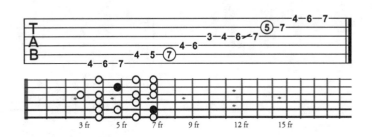

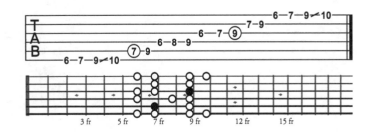

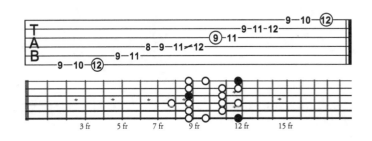

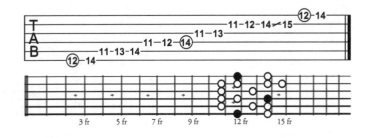

E

# E Super Locrian

**SCALE DEGREES:** 1  ♭2  ♭3  ♭4  ♭5  ♭6  ♭7
**SCALE TONES:**  E  F  G  A♭  B♭  C  D

Super Locrian is the seventh mode of the melodic minor scale. So E Super Locrian is the same as F melodic minor played from E to E.

The "diminished/whole-tone scale," and "altered scale" are two alternate names for this mode.

This mode contains all of the tension tones that can be absorbed in a dominant chord. These tones are the ♭5, ♯5, ♭9, and ♯9.

Use it over E7, E7(♭5), E7(♯5), E7(♭5♭9), E7(♭5♯9), E7(♯11), E7(♭9), E7(♯9), E13(♭9), and E13(♯9).

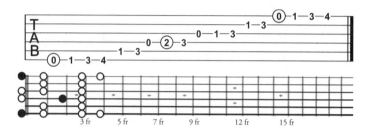

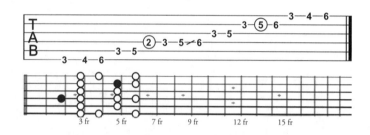

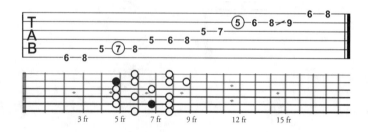

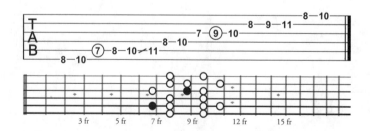

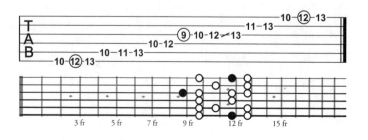

# E Diminished (whole-half)

**SCALE DEGREES:** 1 2 ♭3 4 ♭5 ♯5 6 7
**SCALE TONES:** E F♯ G A B♭ B♯ C♯ D♯

Sometimes called the symmetrical or fully diminished scale, this eight-note scale has some unusual traits. It is useful to understand how the scale is constructed. The primary notes of the scale are those that make up the diminished 7th chord: 1-♭3-♭5-♭♭7. The intervals that occur between these notes are all minor 3rds. The other four notes in this scale are located one half-step below each of these chord tones.

The symmetry in this scale lies in the basic building block of a whole-step followed by a half-step. This "cell" is repeated until the octave is reached.

This symmetry results in the fact that every third note can be considered the root note of the scale. The scale shown here will work with the Edim7, Gdim7, B♭dim7, and C♯dim7 chords. The grey notes in the scale patterns represent these alternate root tones. The scale can be started or ended on either the solid black notes or the grey notes.

Note that the scale pattern repeats itself every three frets, making it quite easy to play at any location on the fingerboard.

# E Diminished (half-whole)

**SCALE DEGREES:** 1 ♭2 ♭3 ♮3 ♯4 5 6 ♭7
**SCALE TONES:** E F G G♯ A♯ B C♯ D

Like the diminished scale (whole-half), this scale is symmetrical. It is the only mode possible in the diminished scale and it is exactly the same as the whole-half diminished scale, except it begins with a half-step instead of a whole-step. The basic building block consists of a half-step followed by a whole-step. This sequence repeats until the octave is reached.

All of this symmetry results in the fact that every third note can be considered the root note of the scale. The scale shown here will work with the E7, E7(♭9), E7(♯9), E7(♭5), E7(♯11), E13(♭9), E7(♭5♭9), and E7(♭5♯9) chords. The only altered dominant chords that don't work with this scale are the ones that contain a ♯5.

The diminished scales are the only eight note scales in common use. Most scales have seven different notes.

The grey notes in the scale patterns represent alternate root tones. The scale can be started or ended on either the solid black notes or the grey notes.

Note that the scale pattern repeats itself every three frets, making it quite easy to play at any location on the fingerboard. Just transpose either of these patterns up or down the fingerboard a distance of three frets.

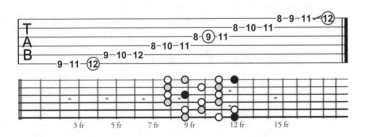

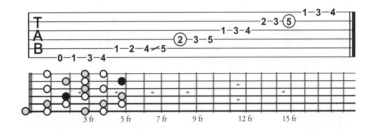

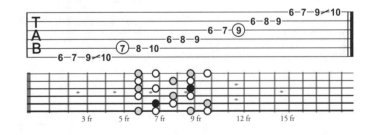

# E Major Pentatonic

**SCALE DEGREES:** 1 2 3 5 6
**SCALE TONES:** E F♯ G♯ B C♯

The major pentatonic scale only has five notes, but it is a scale that is very useful when working in folk, pop, country, and bluegrass styles. This scale avoids the possible dissonance contained in the standard major scale by eliminating the 4th and 7th scale degrees. It can be used over a power chord (E5) as well as Emaj, E6, E6/9, E(add9), Esus2, Emaj7 and Emaj9.

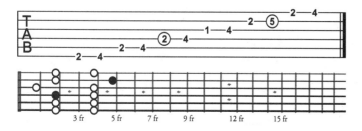

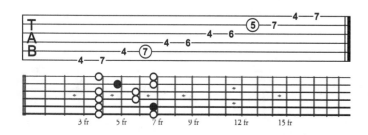

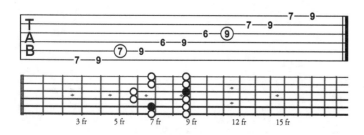

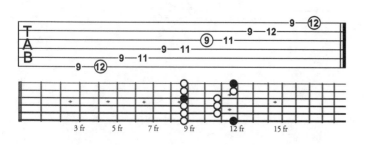

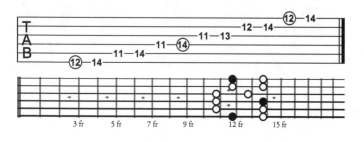

# E Minor Pentatonic

**SCALE DEGREES:** 1 ♭3 4 5 ♭7
**SCALE TONES:** E G A B D

Like the major pentatonic, this scale only contains five notes and is often called the rock scale. It can be traced to the Aeolian (natural minor scale) with two notes removed, the 2nd and 6th.

This scale fits over the power chord (E5) as well as over Em, Em6, Em7, Em6/9, Em(add9), Em11, Em7sus4, Em13, E7, E9, and E7(♯9). In general, use it when you want a rock sound, even if the chord is major.

Since this scale is very similar to the blues scale, they may be used in place of each other.

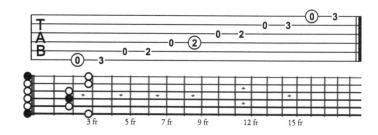

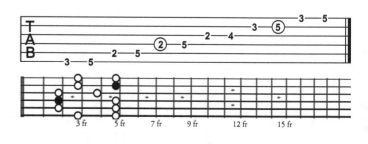

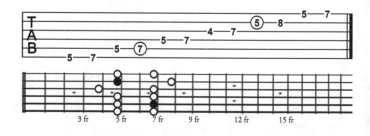

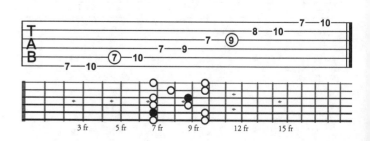

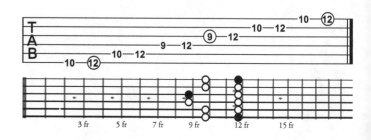

E

# E Blues

**SCALE DEGREES:** 1  ♭3  4  ♯4  5  ♭7
**SCALE TONES:** E  G  A  A♯  B  D

This is a six-note scale and is really just a minor pentatonic with the addition of the ♯4.

Use this scale in the same places where you'd use the minor pentatonic, when you want a bluesy/rock effect.

This scale fits over the power chord (E5) as well as over a wide range of other chords in the minor and dominant categories. Try it over: Em, Em6, Em7, Em6/9, Em(add9), Em11, Em7sus4, Em13, E7, E9, and E7(♯9). It is even played over some major chords. Try it!

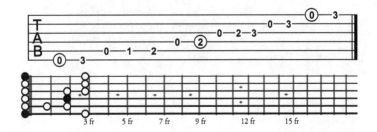

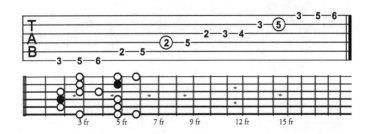

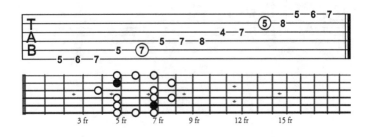

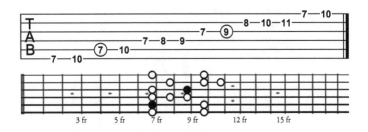

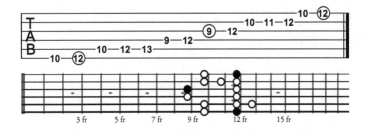

# E Whole Tone

**SCALE DEGREES:**  1  2  3  #4  #5  b7
**SCALE TONES:**  E  F#  G#  A#  B#  D

This six-note scale is probably the easiest to finger of any in this book. What makes it so simple is the fact that the distance from one note to the next is always the same, a whole-step. Because of this symmetry, any note in the scale can actually be called the root. The black dots in these patterns represent E notes, but feel free to start and end on any of the tones in the scale.

Only two fingerings are needed to play this scale since any fingering can be moved up or down the neck in two-fret increments.

The sound of this scale is unlike any other in this book due to the lack of half-steps. This lack of half-steps makes the scale feel very unsettled and void of a tonic note. The feeling is akin to falling through space.

This scale works great with E7(#5), E9(#5), E7(b5), E9(b5), E13(b5), or E13(#5).

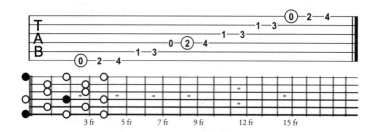

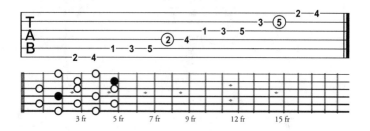

70

The GUITAR SCALE Picture Book

F

Scales and Modes

# F Major

**SCALE DEGREES:** 1 2 3 4 5 6 7
**SCALE TONES:** F G A B♭ C D E

The F major scale (also known as Ionian) can be effectively played over many different F major chords: Fsus2, F6, F6/9, Fmaj7, F(add9) and Fmaj9. If you are going to use it to solo over the simpler F major triad, then you'll want to avoid starting and stopping your solo on the 4th and 7th scale degrees. If you eliminate these two scale degrees from the major scale, you are left with the major pentatonic scale.

# F Dorian

**SCALE DEGREES:** 1 2 ♭3 4 5 6 ♭7
**SCALE TONES:** F G A♭ B♭ C D E♭

Dorian is the second mode of the major scale. So F Dorian is the same as E♭ major, starting and ending on F.

The Dorian mode is a type of minor scale. It is often used when soloing over minor chords and sounds great when played over these chords: Fm, Fm6, Fm6/9, Fm9, Fm7, Fm(add9), Fm11 and Fm13. It is also possible to play it over a F5 (F power chord). Even though the power chord isn't officially a chord at all, the F Dorian mode will still sound cool over it.

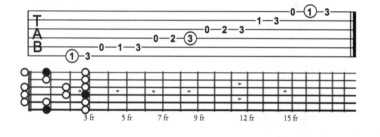

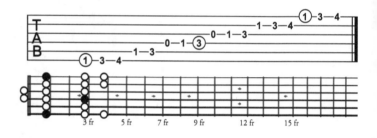

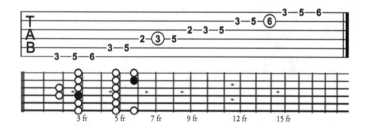

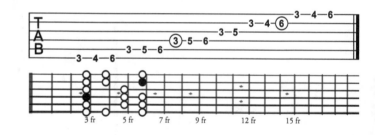

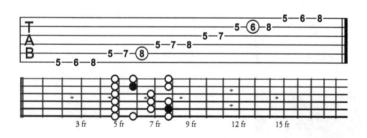

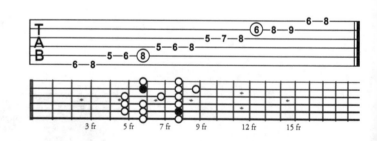

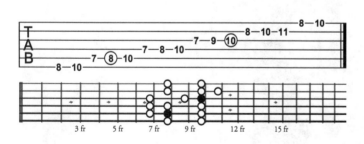

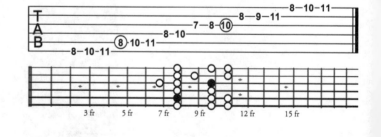

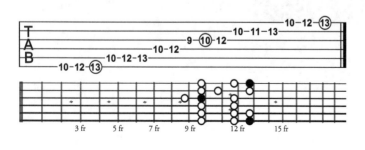

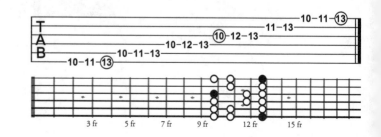

# F Phrygian

SCALE DEGREES: 1  ♭2  ♭3  4  5  ♭6  ♭7
SCALE TONES: F  G♭  A♭  B♭  C  D♭  E♭

Phrygian is the third mode of the major scale. So F Phrygian is the same as D♭ major, starting and ending on F.

The sound is very distinctive due to the fact that it begins with a half-step.

Sometimes called a "Spanish" or flamenco scale, its sound is neither clearly major, minor, nor dominant. It is possible to use it over a Fmaj chord, but it is better suited to Fsus, F7sus, F7sus(♭9). It also sounds good played over the power chord (F5).

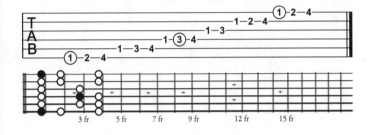

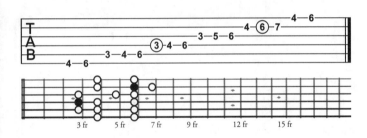

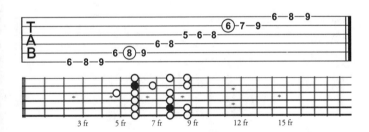

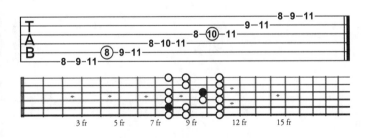

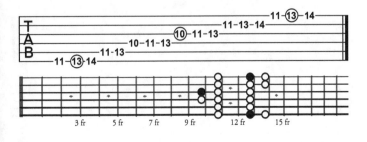

# F Lydian

SCALE DEGREES: 1  2  3  ♯4  5  6  7
SCALE TONES: F  G  A  B  C  D  E

Lydian is the fourth mode of the major scale. So F Lydian is the same as C major, starting and ending on F.

Lydian is the jazz musician's major scale. The inclusion of the ♯4 imparts an urbane and sophisticated sound. The personality of the scale is found in the 3rd, ♯4th and 7th tones. Focus on these notes when playing this scale.

It will work over these chords: Fmaj, F6, Fmaj7(♭5), Fmaj7(♯11), Fmaj9(♭5), Fmaj9(♯11), F6(♭5), F6/9(♭5), and F6/9(♯11). It will also work over the power chord (F5).

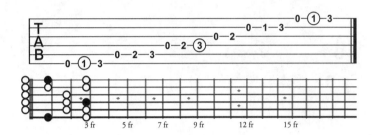

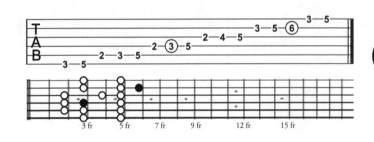

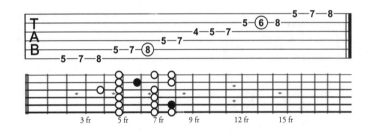

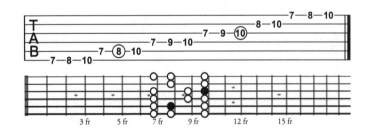

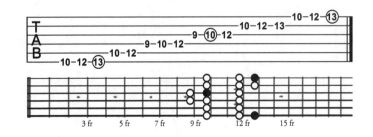

F

73

# F Mixolydian

**SCALE DEGREES:** 1 2 3 4 5 6 ♭7
**SCALE TONES:** F G A B♭ C D E♭

Mixolydian is the fifth mode of the major scale. So F Mixolydian is the same as B♭ major, starting and ending on F.

The Mixolydian mode is a great blues, soul, R&B, and funk scale. It is often used alongside the blues scale when playing over unaltered dominant chords like: F7, F7sus, F9, F9sus, F11, F13, and F13sus. It will also work over the power chord (F5).

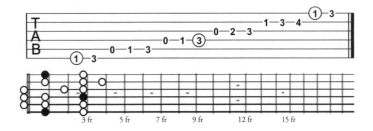

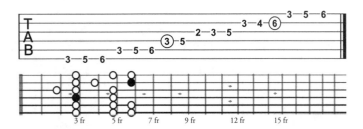

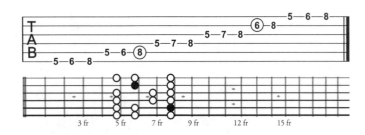

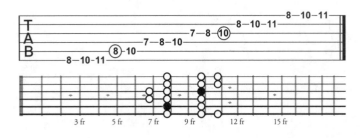

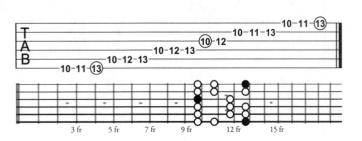

# F Aeolian

**SCALE DEGREES:** 1 2 ♭3 4 5 ♭6 ♭7
**SCALE TONES:** F G A♭ B♭ C D♭ E♭

Aeolian is the sixth mode of the major scale. So F Aeolian is the same as A♭ major, starting and ending on F.

The Aeolian mode is known by several other names: pure minor, natural minor, and relative minor. With so many names you might think this is an important mode, and you'd be correct. This is the mode to use when improvising in minor key songs. It isn't the only scale choice for minor chords (see Dorian, harmonic minor, minor pentatonic and melodic/jazz minor).

In addition to the power chord (F5), this mode will work over Fm, Fm(add9), Fm7, Fm7(♯5), Fm9, and Fm(♯5).

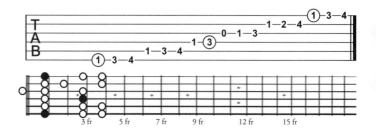

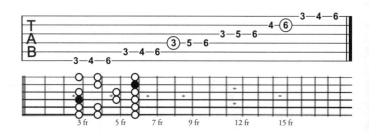

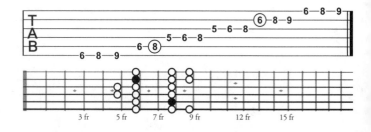

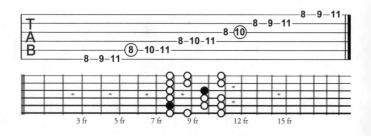

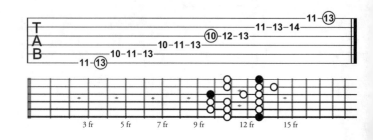

# F Locrian

**SCALE DEGREES:** 1 ♭2 ♭3 4 ♭5 ♭6 ♭7
**SCALE TONES:** F G♭ A♭ B♭ C♭ D♭ E♭

Locrian is the seventh mode of the major scale. So F Locrian is the same as G♭ major, starting and ending on F.

The Locrian mode is the last mode derived from the major scale. It is seldom used in contemporary pop and rock music. Jazz musicians use it when playing over min7(♭5) chords. It has many altered tones, and as such, is unsuitable for use over most other types of minor chords. Use it over Fm7(♭5).

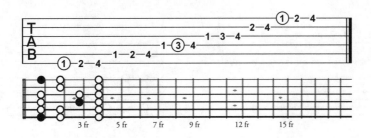

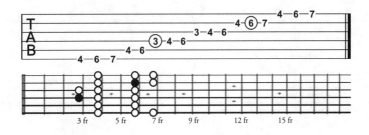

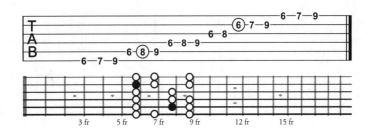

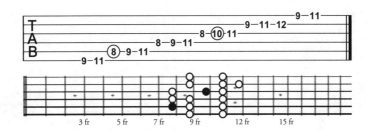

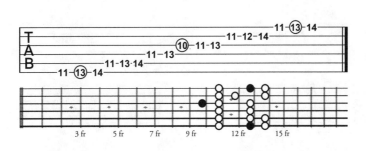

# F Harmonic Minor

**SCALE DEGREES:** 1  2  ♭3  4  5  ♭6  7
**SCALE TONES:**  F  G  A♭  B♭  C  D♭  E

In construction, this scale is very similar to the Aeolian mode. The only difference between the two is the 7th scale degree. The Aeolian has a lowered 7th.

Some people feel that this scale has a Middle Eastern flavor; others sense a Baroque connection. It is a sound adopted by some metal style guitarists.

Use it over Fm, Fm(♯7), Fm(♮7), Fm(add9), Fm7, Fm9(♯7), and Fm9(♮7). It will also work over the F power chord (F5).

# F Phrygian Dominant

**SCALE DEGREES:** 1  ♭2  3  4  5  ♭6  ♭7
**SCALE TONES:**  F  G♭  A  B♭  C  D♭  E♭

Phrygian Dominant is the fifth mode of the harmonic minor scale. So F Phrygian Dominant is the same as B♭ harmonic minor.

It is a scale that is best suited for use when you want to add some tension tones over altered dominant 7th chords. It contains the ♯5 and ♭9 altered tones. These aren't tones you'd typically add to any major or minor chords. It is best suited for F7(♯5), F7(♭9), F13(♭9), and F7(♯5♭9).

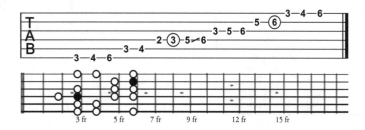

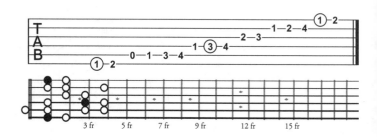

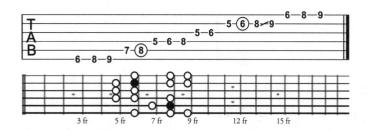

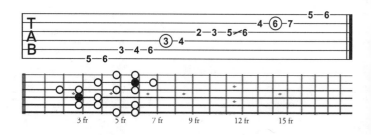

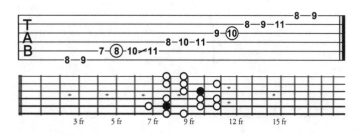

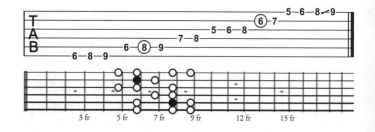

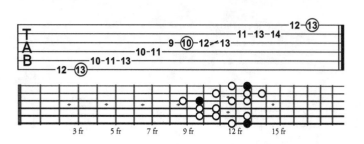

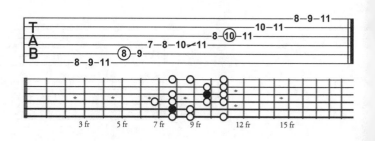

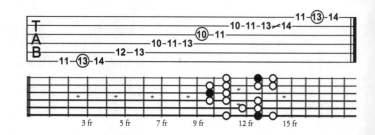

# F Jazz Melodic Minor

**SCALE DEGREES:** 1 2 ♭3 4 5 6 7
**SCALE TONES:** F G A♭ B♭ C D E

There are actually two forms of the melodic minor scale, an ascending form (same as the scale shown here) and a descending form (same notes as the Aeolian mode). For purposes of improvisation, only the ascending version of the scale is used. The term "jazz minor" is used to describe this ascending only version of the scale.

While it is possible to use it over a power chord (F5), this scale is most often played over: Fm, Fm(add9), C#m6, Fm6/9, Fm(#7), Fm(maj7), Fm(add9), Fm6/9(#7), and Fm6/9(maj7).

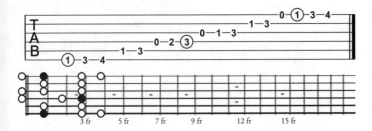

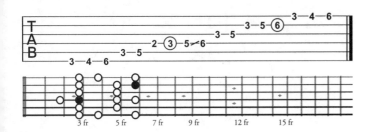

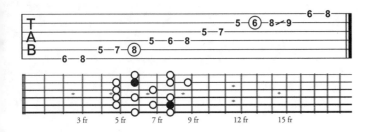

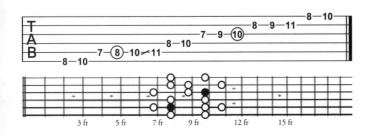

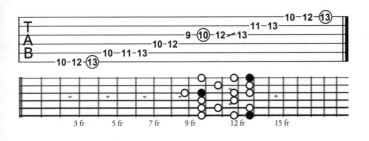

# F Lydian Dominant

**SCALE DEGREES:** 1 2 3 #4 5 6 ♭7
**SCALE TONES:** F G A B C D E♭

Lydian Dominant is the fourth mode of the melodic minor scale. So F Lydian Dominant is the same as C melodic minor played from F to F.

Like some of the other scales, this mode goes by a couple of other names: Mixolydian #4 and Lydian ♭7. It isn't used as a minor scale by improvisers since it is better suited to dominant chords that contain a ♭5 or #11. It is very similar to both the Lydian and Mixolydian modes as the alternate names suggest.

While it is possible to use it over a power chord (F5), this scale is most often played over: F7, F7(♭5), F7(#11), F9, F9(♭5), F9(#11), F13(#11), and F13(♭5).

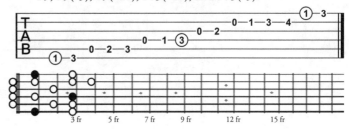

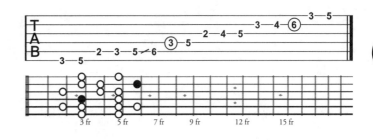

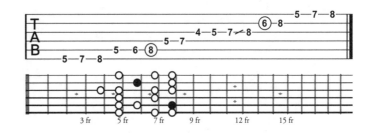

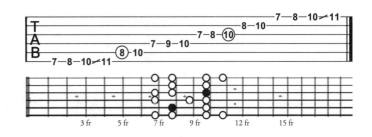

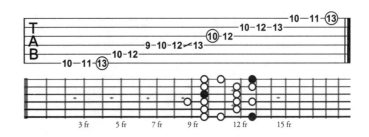

**F**

# F Super Locrian

**SCALE DEGREES:** 1 ♭2 ♭3 ♭4 ♭5 ♭6 ♭7
**SCALE TONES:** F G♭ A♭ B♭♭ C♭ D♭ E♭

Super Locrian is the seventh mode of the melodic minor scale. So F Super Locrian is the same as G♭ melodic minor played from F to F.

The "diminished/whole-tone scale," and "altered scale" are two alternate names for this mode.

This mode contains all of the tension tones that can be absorbed in a dominant chord. These tones are the ♭5, ♯5, ♭9, and ♯9.

Use it over F7, F7(♭5), F7(♯5), F7(♭5♭9), F7(♭5♯9), F7(♯11), F7(♭9), F7(♯9), F13(♭9), and F13(♯9).

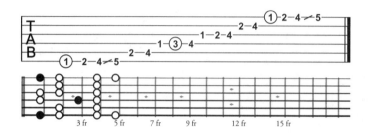

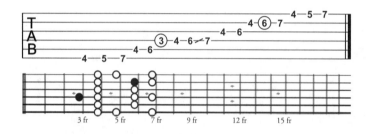

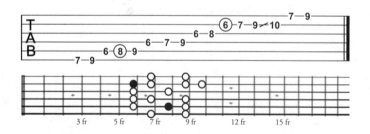

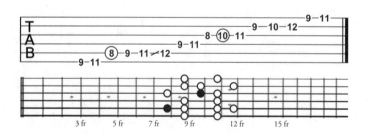

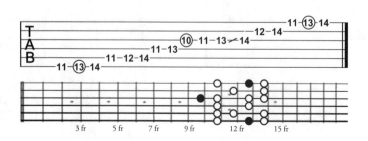

# F Diminished (whole-half)

**SCALE DEGREES:** 1 2 ♭3 4 ♭5 ♯5 6 7
**SCALE TONES:** F G A♭ B♭ C♭ C♯ D E

Sometimes called the symmetrical or fully diminished scale, this eight-note scale has some unusual traits. It is useful to understand how the scale is constructed. The primary notes of the scale are those that make up the diminished 7th chord: 1-♭3-♭5-♭♭7. The intervals that occur between these notes are all minor 3rds. The other four notes in this scale are located one half-step below each of these chord tones.

The symmetry in this scale lies in the basic building block of a whole-step followed by a half-step. This "cell" is repeated until the octave is reached.

This symmetry results in the fact that every third note can be considered the root note of the scale. The scale shown here will work with the Fdim7, A♭dim7, Bdim7, and Ddim7 chords. The grey notes in the scale patterns represent these alternate root tones. The scale can be started or ended on either the solid black notes or the grey notes.

Note that the scale pattern repeats itself every three frets, making it quite easy to play at any location on the fingerboard.

# F Diminished (half-whole)

**SCALE DEGREES:** 1 ♭2 ♭3 ♮3 ♯4 5 6 ♭7
**SCALE TONES:** F G♭ A♭ A♮ B C D E♭

Like the diminished scale (whole-half), this scale is symmetrical. It is the only mode possible in the diminished scale and it is exactly the same as the whole-half diminished scale, except it begins with a half-step instead of a whole-step. The basic building block consists of a half-step followed by a whole-step. This sequence repeats until the octave is reached.

All of this symmetry results in the fact that every third note can be considered the root note of the scale. The scale shown here will work with the F7, F7(♭9), F7(♯9), F7(♭5), F7(♯11), F13(♭9), F7(♭5♭9), and F7(♭5♯9) chords. The only altered dominant chords that don't work with this scale are the ones that contain a ♯5.

The diminished scales are the only eight note scales in common use. Most scales have seven different notes.

The grey notes in the scale patterns represent alternate root tones. The scale can be started or ended on either the solid black notes or the grey notes.

Note that the scale pattern repeats itself every three frets, making it quite easy to play at any location on the fingerboard. Just transpose either of these patterns up or down the fingerboard a distance of three frets.

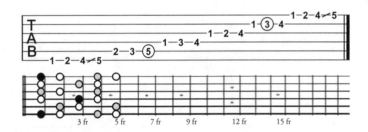

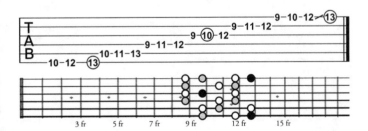

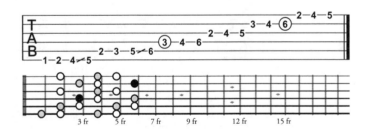

# F Major Pentatonic

**SCALE DEGREES:** 1 2 3 5 6
**SCALE TONES:** F G A C D

The major pentatonic scale only has five notes, but it is a scale that is very useful when working in folk, pop, country, and bluegrass styles. This scale avoids the possible dissonance contained in the standard major scale by eliminating the 4th and 7th scale degrees. It can be used over a power chord (F5) as well as Fmaj, F6, F6/9, F(add9), Fsus2, Fmaj7 and Fmaj9.

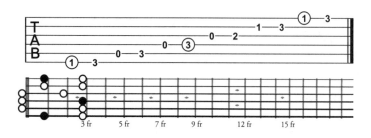

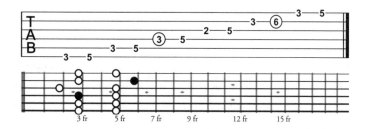

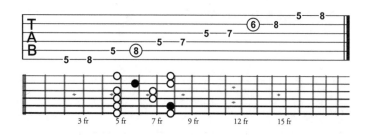

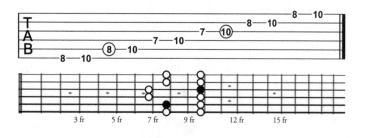

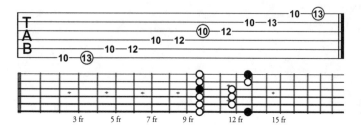

# F Minor Pentatonic

**SCALE DEGREES:** 1 ♭3 4 5 ♭7
**SCALE TONES:** F A♭ B♭ C E♭

Like the major pentatonic, this scale only contains five notes and is often called the rock scale. It can be traced to the Aeolian (natural minor scale) with two notes removed, the 2nd and 6th.

This scale fits over the power chord (F5) as well as over Fm, Fm6, Fm7, Fm6/9, Fm(add9), Fm11, Fm7sus4, Fm13, F7, F9, and F7(♯9). In general, use it when you want a rock sound, even if the chord is major.

Since this scale is very similar to the blues scale, they may be used in place of each other.

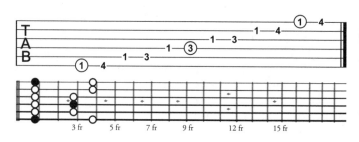

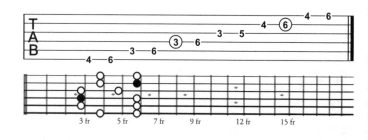

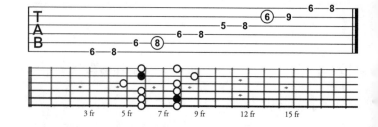

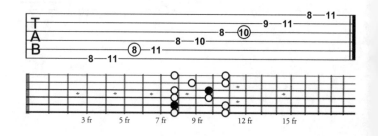

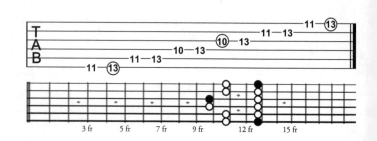

F

# F Blues

**SCALE DEGREES:** 1  ♭3  4  ♯4  5  ♭7
**SCALE TONES:** F  A♭  B♭  B  C  E♭

This is a six-note scale and is really just a minor pentatonic with the addition of the ♯4.

Use this scale in the same places where you'd use the minor pentatonic, when you want a bluesy/rock effect.

This scale fits over the power chord (F5) as well as over a wide range of other chords in the minor and dominant categories. Try it over: Fm, Fm6, Fm7, Fm6/9, Fm(add9), Fm11, Fm7sus4, Fm13, F7, F9, and F7(♯9). It is even played over some major chords. Try it!

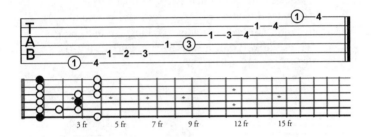

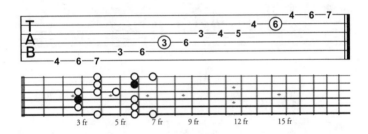

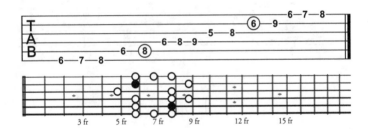

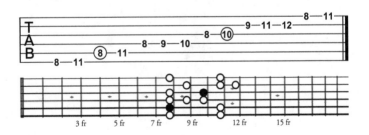

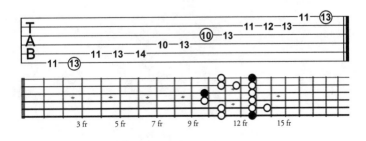

# F Whole Tone

**SCALE DEGREES:** 1   2   3   #4   #5   ♭7
    **SCALE TONES:** F   G   A   B   C#   E♭

This six-note scale is probably the easiest to finger of any in this book. What makes it so simple is the fact that the distance from one note to the next is always the same, a whole-step. Because of this symmetry, any note in the scale can actually be called the root. The black dots in these patterns represent F notes, but feel free to start and end on any of the tones in the scale.

Only two fingerings are needed to play this scale since any fingering can be moved up or down the neck in two-fret increments.

The sound of this scale is unlike any other in this book due to the lack of half-steps. This lack of half-steps makes the scale feel very unsettled and void of a tonic note. The feeling is akin to falling through space.

This scale works great with F7(#5), F9(#5), F7(♭5), F9(♭5), F13(♭5), or F13(#5).

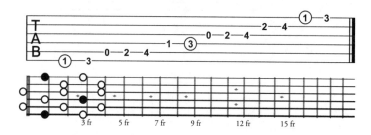

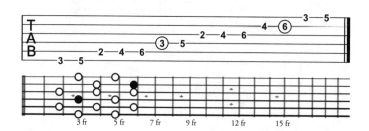

The GUITAR SCALE Picture Book

# F♯/G♭

## Scales and Modes

# F#/G♭ Major

**SCALE DEGREES:** 1 2 3 4 5 6 7
**SCALE TONES:** F# G# A# B C# D# E#

The F# major scale (also known as Ionian) can be effectively played over many different F# major chords: F#sus2, F#6, F#6/9, F#maj7, F#(add9) and F#maj9. If you are going to use it to solo over the simpler F# major triad, then you'll want to avoid starting and stopping your solo on the 4th and 7th scale degrees. If you eliminate these two scale degrees from the major scale, you are left with the major pentatonic scale.

# F#/G♭ Dorian

**SCALE DEGREES:** 1 2 ♭3 4 5 6 ♭7
**SCALE TONES:** F# G# A B C# D# E

Dorian is the second mode of the major scale. So F# Dorian is the same as E major, starting and ending on F#.

The Dorian mode is a type of minor scale. It is often used when soloing over minor chords and sounds great when played over these chords: F#m, F#m6, F#m6/9, F#m9, F#m7, F#m(add9), F#m11 and F#m13. It is also possible to play it over a F#5 (F# power chord). Even though the power chord isn't officially a chord at all, the F# Dorian mode will still sound cool over it.

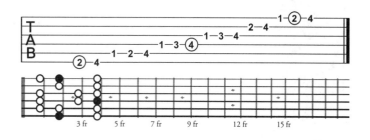

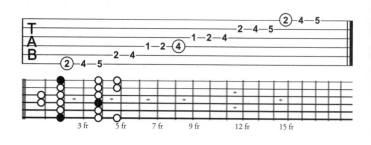

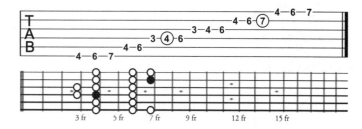

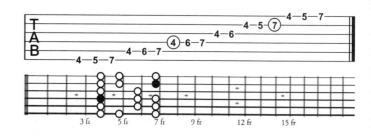

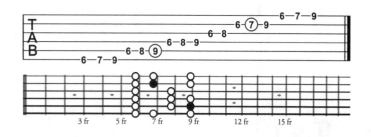

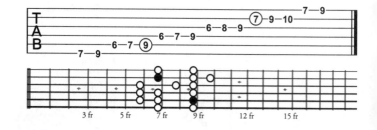

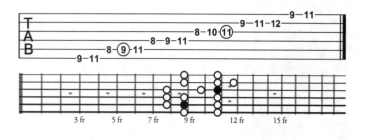

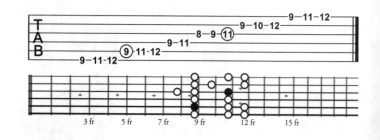

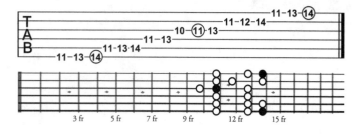

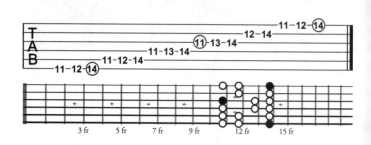

F#
G♭

# F♯/G♭ Phrygian

**SCALE DEGREES:** 1 ♭2 ♭3 4 5 ♭6 ♭7
**SCALE TONES:** F♯ G A B C♯ D E

Phrygian is the third mode of the major scale. So F♯ Phrygian is the same as D major, starting and ending on F♯.

The sound is very distinctive due to the fact that it begins with a half-step.

Sometimes called a "Spanish" or flamenco scale, its sound is neither clearly major, minor, nor dominant. It is possible to use it over a F♯maj chord, but it is better suited to F♯sus, F♯7sus, F♯7sus(♭9). It also sounds good played over the power chord (F♯5).

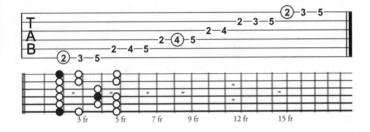

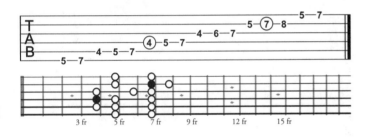

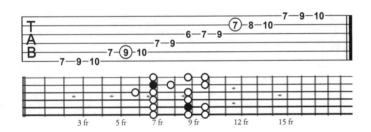

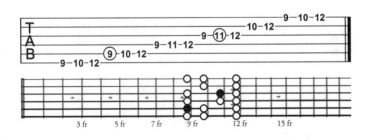

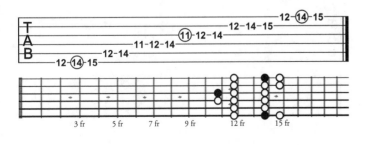

# F♯/G♭ Lydian

**SCALE DEGREES:** 1 2 3 ♯4 5 6 7
**SCALE TONES:** F♯ G♯ A♯ B♯ C♯ D♯ E♯

Lydian is the fourth mode of the major scale. So F♯ Lydian is the same as C♯ major, starting and ending on F♯.

Lydian is the jazz musician's major scale. The inclusion of the ♯4 imparts an urbane and sophisticated sound. The personality of the scale is found in the 3rd, ♯4th and 7th tones. Focus on these notes when playing this scale.

It will work over these chords: F♯maj, F♯6, F♯maj7(♭5), F♯maj7(♯11), F♯maj9(♭5), F♯maj9(♯11), F♯6(♭5), F♯6/9(♭5), and F♯6/9(♯11). It will also work over the power chord (F♯5).

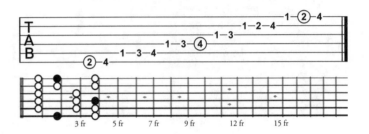

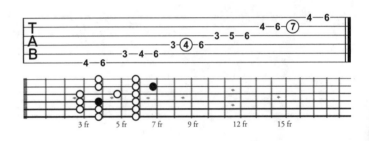

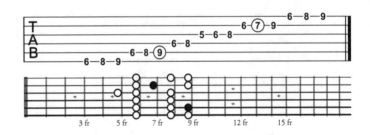

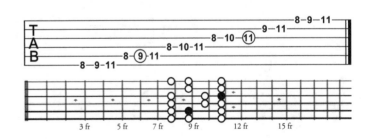

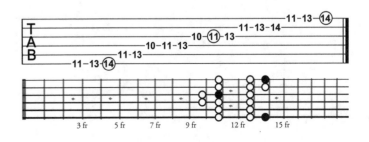

F♯
G♭

85

# F#/Gb Mixolydian

SCALE DEGREES: 1  2  3  4  5  6  b7
SCALE TONES: F#  G#  A#  B  C#  D#  E

Mixolydian is the fifth mode of the major scale. So F# Mixolydian is the same as B major, starting and ending on F#.

The Mixolydian mode is a great blues, soul, R&B, and funk scale. It is often used alongside the blues scale when playing over unaltered dominant chords like: F#7, F#7sus, F#9, F#9sus, F#11, F#13, and F#13sus. It will also work over the power chord (F#5).

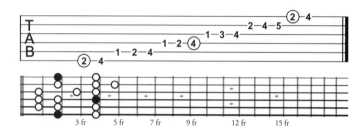

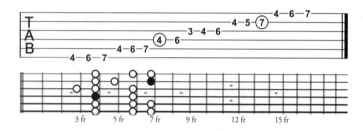

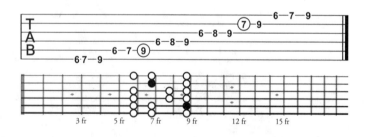

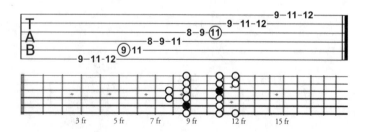

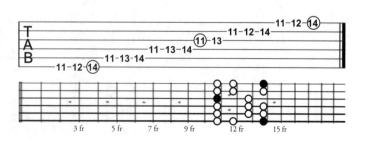

# F#/Gb Aeolian

SCALE DEGREES: 1  2  b3  4  5  b6  b7
SCALE TONES: F#  G#  A  B  C#  D  E

Aeolian is the sixth mode of the major scale. So F# Aeolian is the same as A major, starting and ending on F#.

The Aeolian mode is known by several other names: pure minor, natural minor, and relative minor. With so many names you might think this is an important mode, and you'd be correct. This is the mode to use when improvising in minor key songs. It isn't the only scale choice for minor chords (see Dorian, harmonic minor, minor pentatonic and melodic/jazz minor).

In addition to the power chord (F#5), this mode will work over F#m, F#m(add9), F#m7, F#m7(#5), F#m9, and F#m(#5).

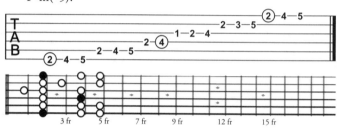

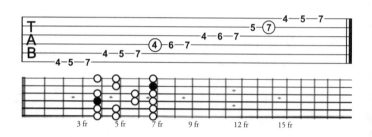

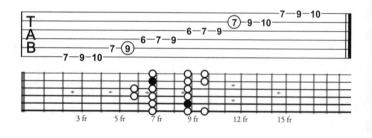

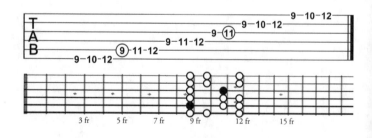

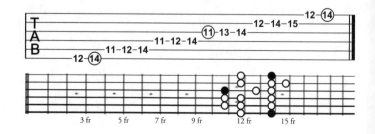

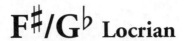

# F#/Gb Locrian

**SCALE DEGREES:** 1 ♭2 ♭3 4 ♭5 ♭6 ♭7
**SCALE TONES:** F# G A B C D E

Locrian is the seventh mode of the major scale. So F# Locrian is the same as G major, starting and ending on F#.

The Locrian mode is the last mode derived from the major scale. It is seldom used in contemporary pop and rock music. Jazz musicians use it when playing over min7(♭5) chords. It has many altered tones, and as such, is unsuitable for use over most other types of minor chords. Use it over F#m7(♭5).

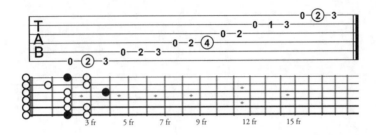

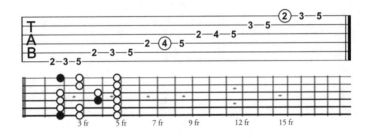

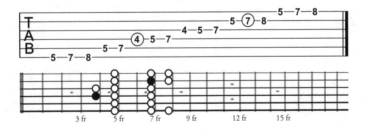

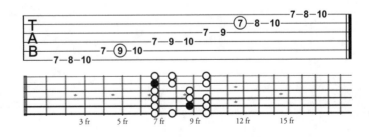

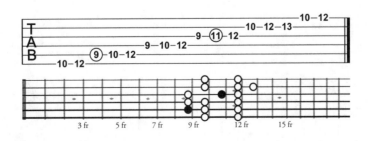

# F#/G♭ Harmonic Minor

**SCALE DEGREES:** 1 2 ♭3 4 5 ♭6 7
**SCALE TONES:** F# G# A B C# D E#

In construction, this scale is very similar to the Aeolian mode. The only difference between the two is the 7th scale degree. The Aeolian has a lowered 7th.

Some people feel that this scale has a Middle Eastern flavor; others sense a Baroque connection. It is a sound adopted by some metal-style guitarists.

Use it over F#m, F#m(#7), F#m(maj7), F#m(add9), F#m7, F#m9(maj7), and F#m9(♭7). It will also work over the F# power chord (F#5).

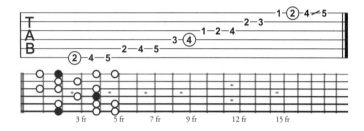

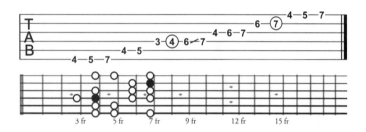

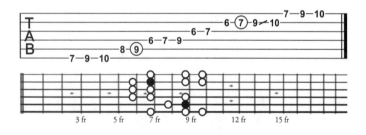

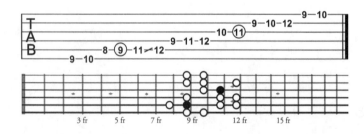

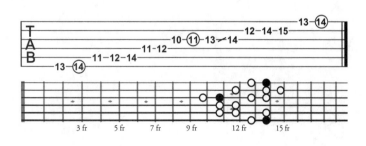

# F#/G♭ Phrygian Dominant

**SCALE DEGREES:** 1 ♭2 3 4 5 ♭6 ♭7
**SCALE TONES:** F# G A# B C# D E

Phrygian Dominant is the fifth mode of the harmonic minor scale. So F# Phrygian Dominant is the same as B harmonic minor.

It is a scale that is best suited for use when you want to add some tension tones over altered dominant 7th chords. It contains the #5 and ♭9 altered tones. These aren't tones you'd typically add to any major or minor chords. It is best suited for F#7(#5), F#7(♭9), F#13(♭9), and F#7(#5♭9).

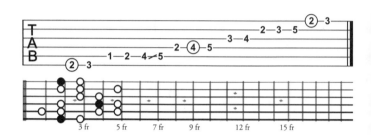

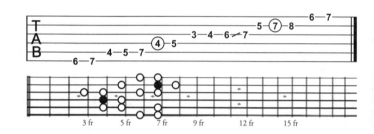

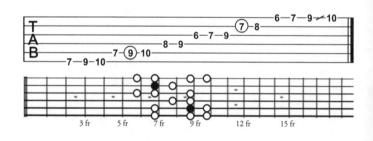

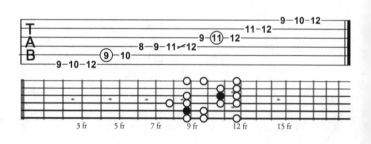

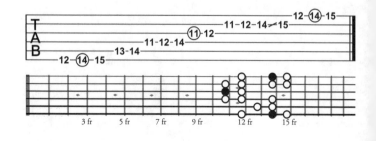

# F#/Gb Jazz Melodic Minor

SCALE DEGREES: 1  2  b3  4  5  6  7
SCALE TONES: F#  G#  A  B  C#  D#  E#

There are actually two forms of the melodic minor scale, an ascending form (same as the scale shown here) and a descending form (same notes as the Aeolian mode). For purposes of improvisation, only the ascending version of the scale is used. The term "jazz minor" is used to describe this ascending only version of the scale.

While it is possible to use it over a power chord (F#5), this scale is most often played over: F#m, F#m(add9), F#m6, F#m6/9, F#m(#7), F#m(maj7), F#m(add9), F#m6/9(#7), and F#m6/9(maj7).

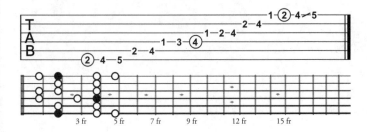

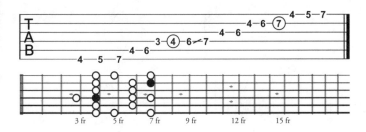

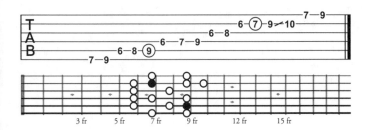

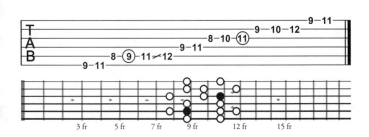

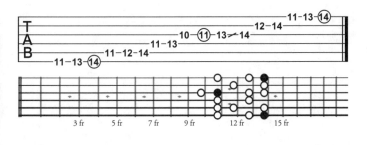

# F#/Gb Lydian Dominant

SCALE DEGREES: 1  2  3  #4  5  6  b7
SCALE TONES: F#  G#  A#  B#  C#  D#  E

Lydian Dominant is the fourth mode of the melodic minor scale. So F# Lydian Dominant is the same as C# melodic minor played from F# to F#.

Like some of the other scales, this mode goes by a couple of other names: Mixolydian #4 and Lydian b7. It isn't used as a minor scale by improvisers since it is better suited to dominant chords that contain a b5 or #11. It is very similar to both the Lydian and Mixolydian modes as the alternate names suggest.

While it is possible to use it over a power chord (F#5), this scale is most often played over: F#7, F#7(b5), F#7(#11), F#9, F#9(b5), F#9(#11), F#13(#11), and F#13(b5).

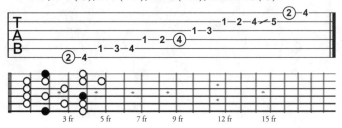

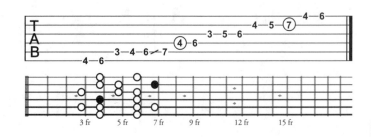

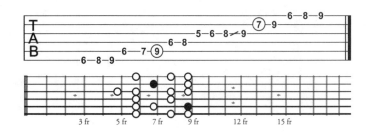

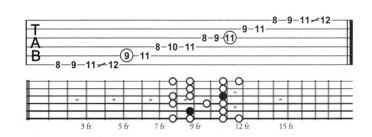

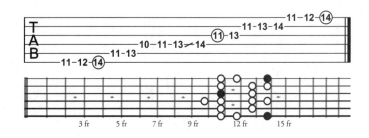

# F♯/G♭ Super Locrian

**SCALE DEGREES:** 1 ♭2 ♭3 ♭4 ♭5 ♭6 ♭7
**SCALE TONES:** F♯ G A B♭ C D E

Super Locrian is the seventh mode of the melodic minor scale. So F♯ Super Locrian is the same as G melodic minor played from F♯ to F♯.

The "diminished/whole-tone scale," and "altered scale" are two alternate names for this mode.

This mode contains all of the tension tones that can be absorbed in a dominant chord. These tones are the ♭5, ♯5, ♭9, and ♯9.

Use it over F♯7, F♯7(♭5), F♯7(♯5), F♯7(♭5♭9), F♯7(♭5♯9), F♯7(♯11), F♯7(♭9), F♯7(♯9), F♯13(♭9), and F♯13(♯9).

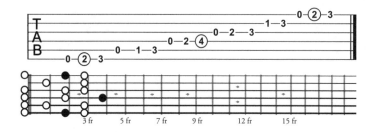

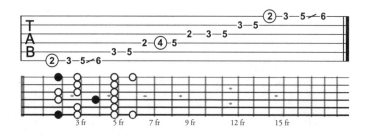

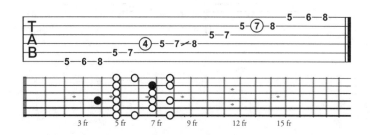

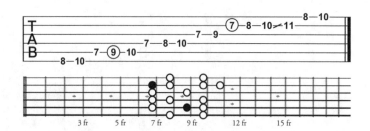

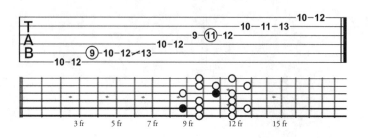

# F♯/G♭ Diminished (whole-half)

**SCALE DEGREES:** 1 2 ♭3 4 ♭5 ♯5 6 7
**SCALE TONES:** F♯ G♯ A B C C✕ D♯ E✕

Sometimes called the symmetrical or fully diminished scale, this eight-note scale has some unusual traits. It is useful to understand how the scale is constructed. The primary notes of the scale are those that make up the diminished 7th chord: 1-♭3-♭5-♭♭7. The intervals that occur between these notes are all minor 3rds. The other four notes in this scale are located one half-step below each of these chord tones.

The symmetry in this scale lies in the basic building block of a whole-step followed by a half-step. This "cell" is repeated until the octave is reached.

This symmetry results in the fact that every third note can be considered the root note of the scale. The scale shown here will work with the F♯dim7, Adim7, Cdim7, and E♭dim7 chords. The grey notes in the scale patterns represent these alternate root tones. The scale can be started or ended on either the solid black notes or the grey notes.

Note that the scale pattern repeats itself every three frets, making it quite easy to play at any location on the fingerboard.

# F♯/G♭ Diminished (half-whole)

**SCALE DEGREES:** 1 ♭2 ♭3 ♮3 ♯4 5 6 ♭7
**SCALE TONES:** F♯ G A A♯ B♯ C♯ D♯ E

Like the diminished scale (whole-half), this scale is symmetrical. It is the only mode possible in the diminished scale and it is exactly the same as the whole-half diminished scale, except it begins with a half-step instead of a whole-step. The basic building block consists of a half-step followed by a whole-step. This sequence repeats until the octave is reached.

All of this symmetry results in the fact that every third note can be considered the root note of the scale. The scale shown here will work with the F♯7, F♯7(♭9), F♯7(♯9), F♯7(♭5), F♯7(♯11), F♯13(♭9), F♯7(♭5♭9), and F♯7(♭5♯9) chords. The only altered dominant chords that don't work with this scale are the ones that contain a ♯5.

The diminished scales are the only eight note scales in common use. Most scales have seven different notes.

The grey notes in the scale patterns represent alternate root tones. The scale can be started or ended on either the solid black notes or the grey notes.

Note that the scale pattern repeats itself every three frets, making it quite easy to play at any location on the fingerboard. Just transpose either of these patterns up or down the fingerboard a distance of three frets.

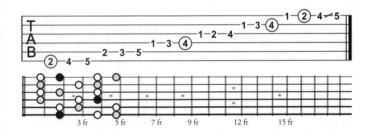

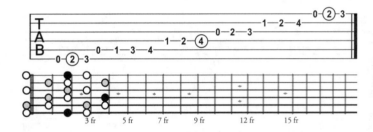

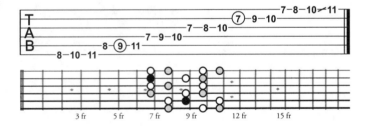

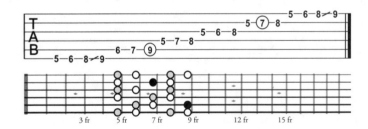

# F#/G♭ Major Pentatonic

**SCALE DEGREES:** 1 2 3 5 6
**SCALE TONES:** F# G# A# C# D#

The major pentatonic scale only has five notes, but it is a scale that is very useful when working in folk, pop, country, and bluegrass styles. This scale avoids the possible dissonance contained in the standard major scale by eliminating the 4th and 7th scale degrees. It can be used over a power chord (F#5) as well as F#maj, F#6, F#6/9, F#(add9), F#sus2, F#maj7 and F#maj9.

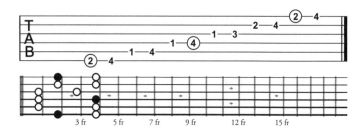

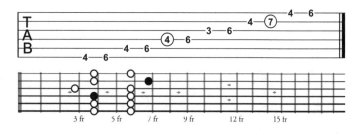

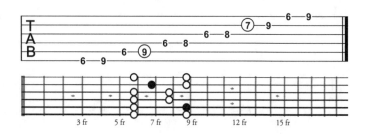

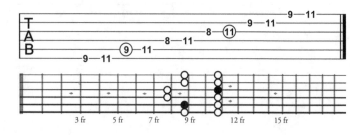

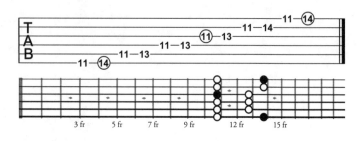

# F#/G♭ Minor Pentatonic

**SCALE DEGREES:** 1 ♭3 4 5 ♭7
**SCALE TONES:** F# A B C# E

Like the major pentatonic, this scale only contains five notes and is often called the rock scale. It can be traced to the Aeolian (natural minor scale) with two notes removed, the 2nd and 6th.

This scale fits over the power chord (F#5) as well as over F#m, F#m6, F#m7, F#m6/9, F#m(add9), F#m11, F#m7sus4, F#m13, F#7, F#9, and F#7(#9). In general, use it when you want a rock sound, even if the chord is major.

Since this scale is very similar to the blues scale, they may be used in place of each other.

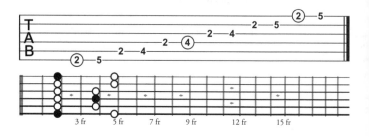

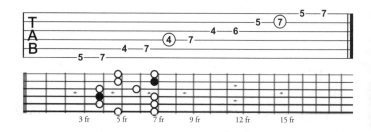

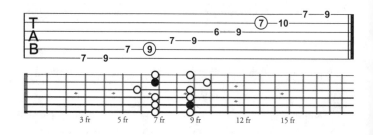

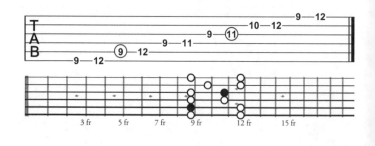

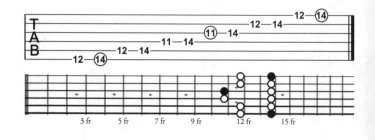

F#
G♭

# F#/G♭ Blues

**SCALE DEGREES:** 1 ♭3 4 ♯4 5 ♭7
**SCALE TONES:** F♯ A B B♯ C♯ E

This is a six-note scale and is really just a minor pentatonic with the addition of the ♯4.

Use this scale in the same places where you'd use the minor pentatonic, when you want a bluesy/rock effect.

This scale fits over the power chord (F♯5) as well as over a wide range of other chords in the minor and dominant categories. Try it over: F♯m, F♯m6, F♯m7, F♯m6/9, F♯m(add9), F♯m11, F♯m7sus4, F♯m13, F♯7, F♯9, and F♯7(♯9). It is even played over some major chords. Try it!

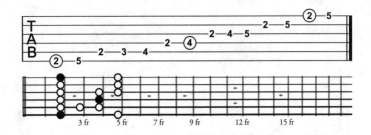

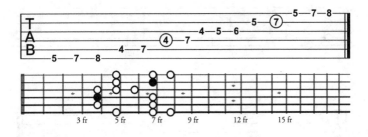

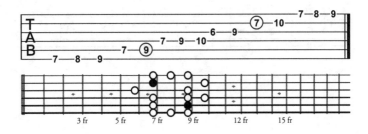

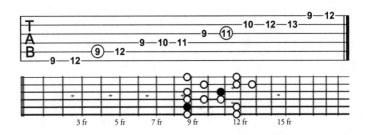

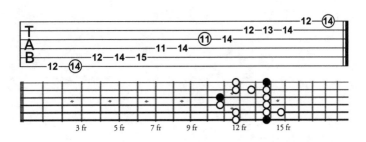

# F♯/G♭ Whole Tone

**SCALE DEGREES:** 1 2 3 ♯4 ♯5 ♭7
**SCALE TONES:** G♭ A♭ B♭ C D F♭

This six-note scale is probably the easiest to finger of any in this book. What makes it so simple is the fact that the distance from one note to the next is always the same, a whole-step. Because of this symmetry, any note in the scale can actually be called the root. The black dots in these patterns represent G♭ notes, but feel free to start and end on any of the tones in the scale.

Only two fingerings are needed to play this scale since any fingering can be moved up or down the neck in two-fret increments.

The sound of this scale is unlike any other in this book due to the lack of half-steps. This lack of half-steps makes the scale feel very unsettled and void of a tonic note. The feeling is akin to falling through space.

This scale works great with G♭7(♯5), G♭9(♯5), G♭7(♭5), G♭9(♭5), G♭13(♭5), or G♭13(♯5).

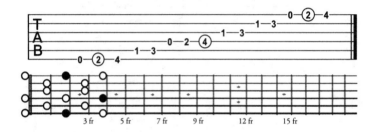

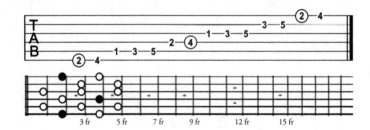

The GUITAR SCALE Picture Book

# G

### Scales and Modes

# G Major

**SCALE DEGREES:** 1  2  3  4  5  6  7
**SCALE TONES:** G  A  B  C  D  E  F#

The G major scale (also known as Ionian) can be effectively played over many different G major chords: Gsus2, G6, G6/9, Gmaj7, G(add9) and Gmaj9. If you are going to use it to solo over the simpler G major triad, then you'll want to avoid starting and stopping your solo on the 4th and 7th scale degrees. If you eliminate these two scale degrees from the major scale, you are left with the major pentatonic scale.

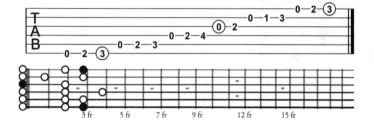

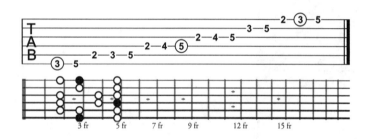

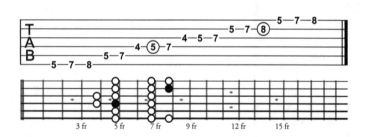

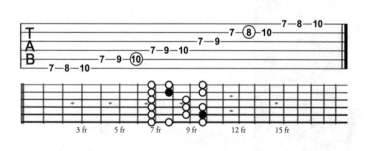

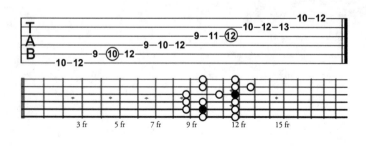

# G Dorian

**SCALE DEGREES:** 1  2  ♭3  4  5  6  ♭7
**SCALE TONES:** G  A  B♭  C  D  E  F

Dorian is the second mode of the major scale. So G Dorian is the same as F major, starting and ending on G.

The Dorian mode is a type of minor scale. It is often used when soloing over minor chords and sounds great when played over these chords: Gm, Gm6, Gm6/9, Gm9, Gm7, Gm(add9), Gm11 and Gm13. It is also possible to play it over a G5 (G power chord). Even though the power chord isn't officially a chord at all, the G Dorian mode will still sound cool over it.

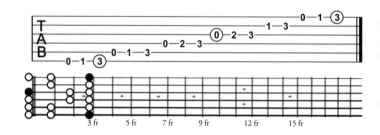

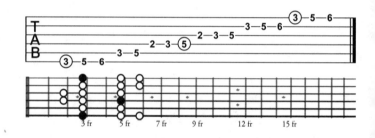

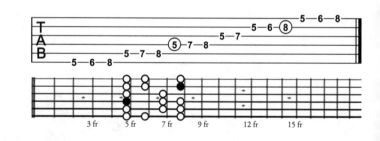

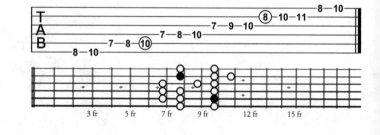

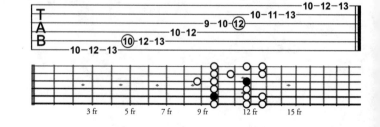

# G Phrygian

**SCALE DEGREES:** 1 ♭2 ♭3 4 5 ♭6 ♭7
**SCALE TONES:** G A♭ B♭ C D E♭ F

Phrygian is the third mode of the major scale. So G Phrygian is the same as E♭ major, starting and ending on G.

The sound is very distinctive due to the fact that it begins with a half-step.

Sometimes called a "Spanish" or flamenco scale, its sound is neither clearly major, minor, nor dominant. It is possible to use it over a Gmaj chord, but it is better suited to Gsus, G7sus, G7sus(♭9). It also sounds good played over the power chord (G5).

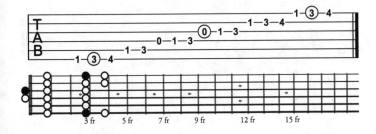

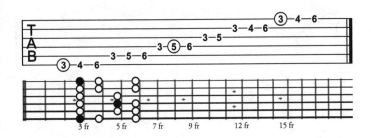

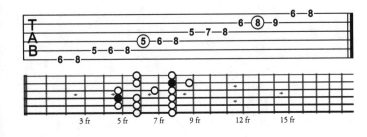

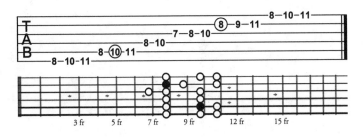

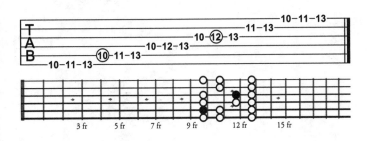

# G Lydian

**SCALE DEGREES:** 1 2 3 #4 5 6 7
**SCALE TONES:** G A B C# D E F#

Lydian is the fourth mode of the major scale. So G Lydian is the same as D major, starting and ending on G.

Lydian is the jazz musician's major scale. The inclusion of the #4 imparts an urbane and sophisticated sound. The personality of the scale is found in the 3rd, #4th and 7th tones. Focus on these notes when playing this scale.

It will work over these chords: Gmaj, G6, Gmaj7(♭5), Gmaj7(#11), Gmaj9(♭5), Gmaj9(#11), G6(♭5), G6/9(♭5), and G6/9(#11). It will also work over the power chord (G5).

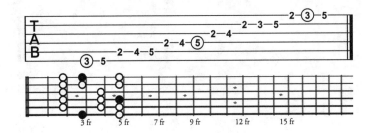

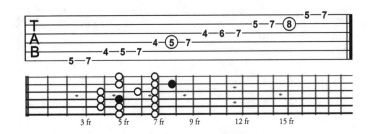

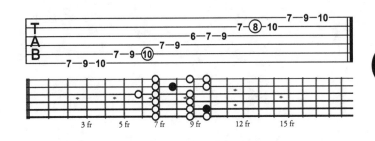

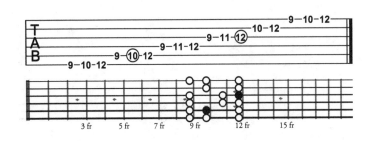

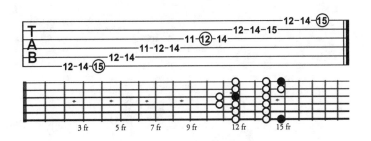

# G Mixolydian

**SCALE DEGREES:** 1 2 3 4 5 6 ♭7
**SCALE TONES:** G A B C D E F

Mixolydian is the fifth mode of the major scale. So G Mixolydian is the same as C major, starting and ending on G.

The Mixolydian mode is a great blues, soul, R&B, and funk scale. It is often used alongside the blues scale when playing over unaltered dominant chords like: G7, G7sus, G9, G9sus, G11, G13, and G13sus. It will also work over the power chord (G5).

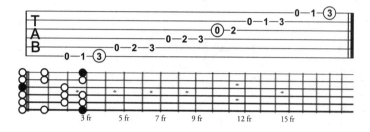

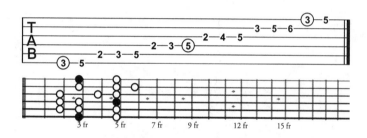

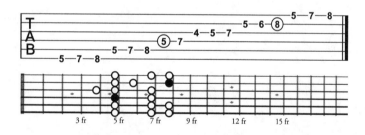

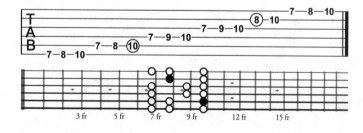

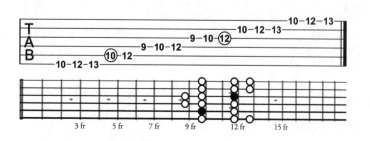

# G Aeolian

**SCALE DEGREES:** 1 2 ♭3 4 5 ♭6 ♭7
**SCALE TONES:** G A B♭ C D E♭ F

Aeolian is the sixth mode of the major scale. So G Aeolian is the same as B♭ major, starting and ending on G.

The Aeolian mode is known by several other names: pure minor, natural minor, and relative minor. With so many names you might think this is an important mode, and you'd be correct. This is the mode to use when improvising in minor key songs. It isn't the only scale choice for minor chords (see Dorian, harmonic minor, minor pentatonic and melodic/jazz minor).

In addition to the power chord (G5), this mode will work over Gm, Gm(add9), Gm7, Gm7(♯5), Gm9, and Gm(♯5).

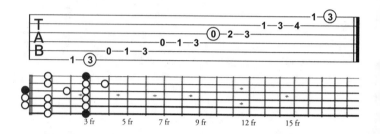

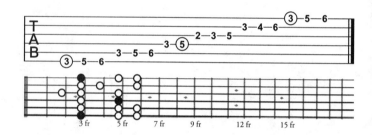

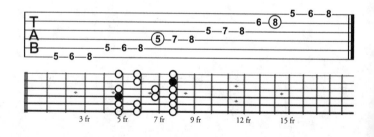

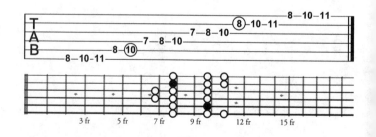

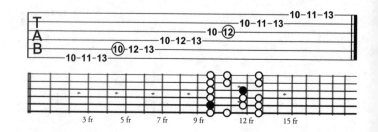

# G Locrian

**SCALE DEGREES:** 1  ♭2  ♭3  4  ♭5  ♭6  ♭7
**SCALE TONES:** G  A♭  B♭  C  D♭  E♭  F

Locrian is the seventh mode of the major scale. So G Locrian is the same as A♭ major, starting and ending on G.

The Locrian mode is the last mode derived from the major scale. It is seldom used in contemporary pop and rock music. Jazz musicians use it when playing over min7(♭5) chords. It has many altered tones, and as such, is unsuitable for use over most other types of minor chords. Use it over Gm7(♭5).

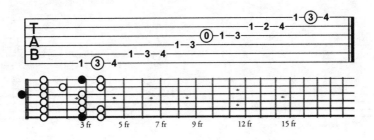

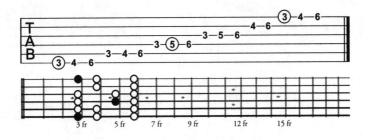

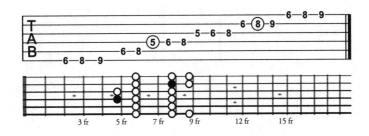

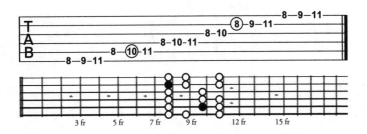

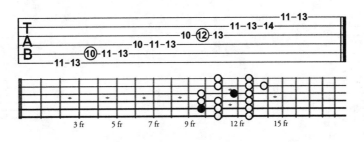

# G Harmonic Minor

**SCALE DEGREES:** 1  2  ♭3  4  5  ♭6  7
**SCALE TONES:**  G  A  B♭  C  D  E♭  F♯

In construction, this scale is very similar to the Aeolian mode. The only difference between the two is the 7th scale degree. The Aeolian has a lowered 7th.

Some people feel that this scale has a Middle Eastern flavor; others sense a Baroque connection. It is a sound adopted by some metal-style guitarists.

Use it over Gm, Gm(♯7), Gm(maj7), Gm(add9), Gm7, Gm9(maj7), and Gm9(♯7). It will also work over the G power chord (G5).

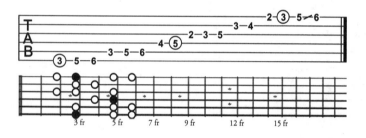

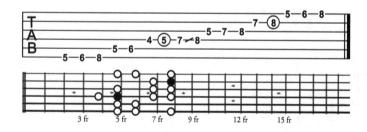

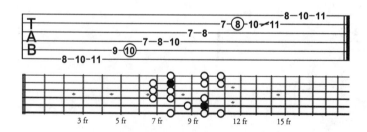

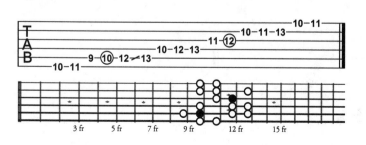

# G Phrygian Dominant

**SCALE DEGREES:** 1  ♭2  3  4  5  ♭6  ♭7
**SCALE TONES:**  G  A♭  B  C  D  E♭  F

Phrygian Dominant is the 5th mode of the harmonic minor scale. So G Phrygian Dominant is the same as C harmonic minor.

It is a scale that is best suited for use when you want to add some tension tones over altered dominant 7th chords. It contains the ♯5 and ♭9 altered tones. These aren't tones you'd typically add to any major or minor chords. It is best suited for G7(♯5), G7(♭9), G13(♭9), and G7(♯5♭9).

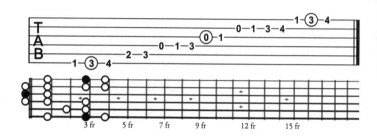

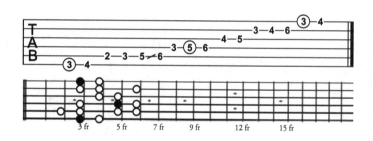

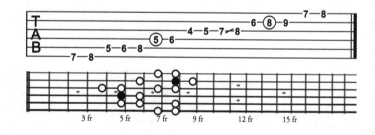

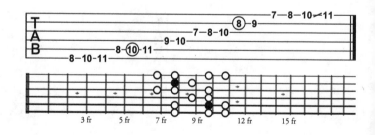

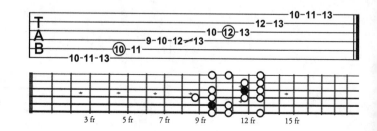

# G Jazz Melodic Minor

SCALE DEGREES: 1 2 ♭3 4 5 6 7
SCALE TONES: G A B♭ C D E F♯

There are actually two forms of the melodic minor scale, an ascending form (same as the scale shown here) and a descending form (same notes as the Aeolian mode). For purposes of improvisation, only the ascending version of the scale is used. The term "jazz minor" is used to describe this ascending only version of the scale.

While it is possible to use it over a power chord (G5), this scale is most often played over: Gm, Gm(add9), Gm6, Gm6/9, Gm(♯7), Gm(maj7), Gm(add9), Gm6/9(♯7), and Gm6/9(maj7).

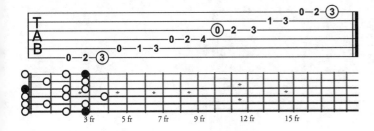

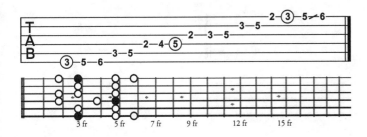

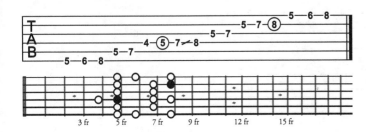

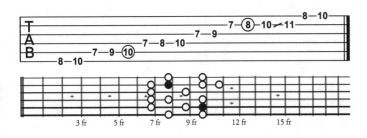

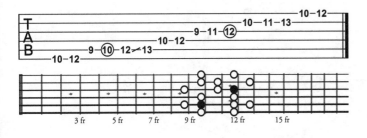

# G Lydian Dominant

SCALE DEGREES: 1 2 3 ♯4 5 6 ♭7
SCALE TONES: G A B C♯ D E F

Lydian Dominant is the fourth mode of the melodic minor scale. So G Lydian Dominant is the same as D melodic minor played from G to G.

Like some of the other scales, this mode goes by a couple of other names: Mixolydian ♯4 and Lydian ♭7. It isn't used as a minor scale by improvisers since it is better suited to dominant chords that contain a ♭5 or ♯11. It is very similar to both the Lydian and Mixolydian modes as the alternate names suggest.

While it is possible to use it over a power chord (G5), this scale is most often played over: G7, G7(♭5), G7(♯11), G9, G9(♭5), G9(♯11), G13(♯11), and G13(♭5).

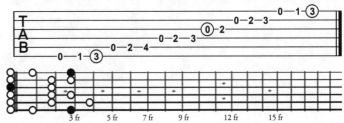

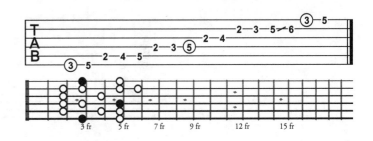

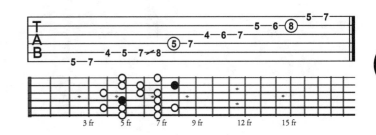

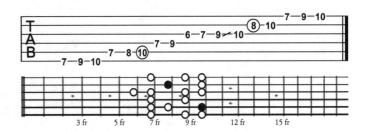

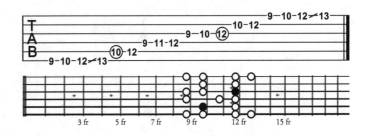

G

# G Super Locrian

SCALE DEGREES: 1 ♭2 ♭3 ♭4 ♭5 ♭6 ♭7
SCALE TONES: G A♭ B♭ C♭ D♭ E♭ F

Super Locrian is the seventh mode of the melodic minor scale. So G Super Locrian is the same as A♭ melodic minor played from G to G.

The "diminished/whole-tone scale," and "altered scale" are two alternate names for this mode.

This mode contains all of the tension tones that can be absorbed in a dominant chord. These tones are the ♭5, ♯5, ♭9, and ♯9.

Use it over G7, G7(♭5), G7(♯5), G7(♭5♭9), G7(♭5♯9), G7(♯11), G7(♭9), G7(♯9), G13(♭9), and G13(♯9).

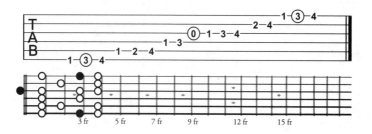

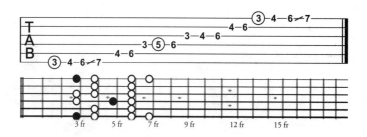

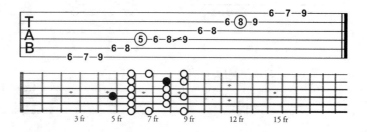

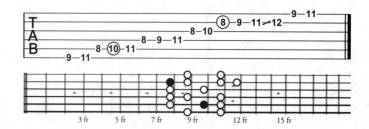

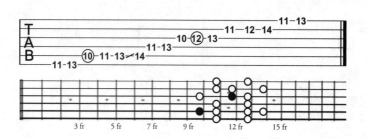

# G Diminished (whole-half)

**SCALE DEGREES:** 1 2 ♭3 4 ♭5 ♯5 6 7
**SCALE TONES:** G A B♭ C D♭ D♯ E F♯

Sometimes called the symmetrical or fully diminished scale, this eight-note scale has some unusual traits. It is useful to understand how the scale is constructed. The primary notes of the scale are those that make up the diminished 7th chord: 1-♭3-♭5-♭♭7. The intervals that occur between these notes are all minor 3rds. The other four notes in this scale are located one half-step below each of these chord tones.

The symmetry in this scale lies in the basic building block of a whole-step followed by a half-step. This "cell" is repeated until the octave is reached.

This symmetry results in the fact that every third note can be considered the root note of the scale. The scale shown here will work with the Gdim7, B♭dim7, C♯dim7, and Edim7 chords. The grey notes in the scale patterns represent these alternate root tones. The scale can be started or ended on either the solid black notes or the grey notes.

Note that the scale pattern repeats itself every three frets, making it quite easy to play at any location on the fingerboard.

# G Diminished (half-whole)

**SCALE DEGREES:** 1 ♭2 ♭3 ♮3 ♯4 5 6 ♭7
**SCALE TONES:** G A♭ B♭ B♮ C♯ D E F

Like the diminished scale (whole-half), this scale is symmetrical. It is the only mode possible in the diminished scale and it is exactly the same as the whole-half diminished scale, except it begins with a half-step instead of a whole-step. The basic building block consists of a half-step followed by a whole-step. This sequence repeats until the octave is reached.

All of this symmetry results in the fact that every third note can be considered the root note of the scale. The scale shown here will work with the G7, G7(♭9), G7(♯9), G7(♭5), G7(♯11), G13(♭9), G7(♭5♭9), and G7(♭5♯9) chords. The only altered dominant chords that don't work with this scale are the ones that contain a ♯5.

The diminished scales are the only eight note scales in common use. Most scales have seven different notes.

The grey notes in the scale patterns represent alternate root tones. The scale can be started or ended on either the solid black notes or the grey notes.

Note that the scale pattern repeats itself every three frets, making it quite easy to play at any location on the fingerboard. Just transpose either of these patterns up or down the fingerboard a distance of three frets.

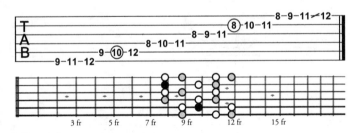

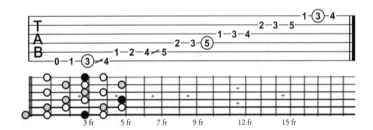

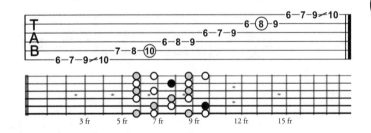

# G Major Pentatonic

**SCALE DEGREES:** 1 2 3 5 6
**SCALE TONES:** G A B D E

The major pentatonic scale only has five notes, but it is a scale that is very useful when working in folk, pop, country, and bluegrass styles. This scale avoids the possible dissonance contained in the standard major scale by eliminating the 4th and 7th scale degrees. It can be used over a power chord (G5) as well as Gmaj, G6, G6/9, G(add9), Gsus2, Gmaj7 and Gmaj9.

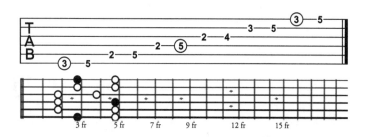

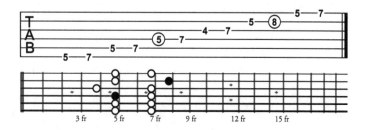

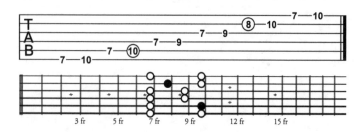

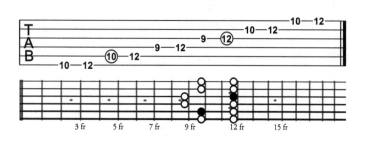

# G Minor Pentatonic

**SCALE DEGREES:** 1 ♭3 4 5 ♭7
**SCALE TONES:** G B♭ C D F

Like the major pentatonic, this scale only contains five notes and is often called the rock scale. It can be traced to the Aeolian (natural minor scale) with two notes removed, the 2nd and 6th.

This scale fits over the power chord (G5) as well as over Gm, Gm6, Gm7, Gm6/9, Gm(add9), Gm11, Gm7sus4, Gm13, G7, G9, and G7(♯9). In general, use it when you want a rock sound, even if the chord is major.

Since this scale is very similar to the blues scale, they may be used in place of each other.

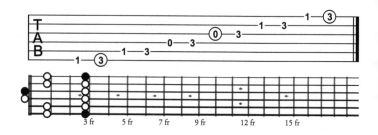

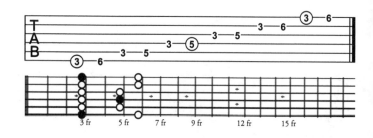

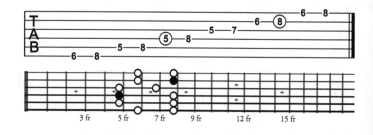

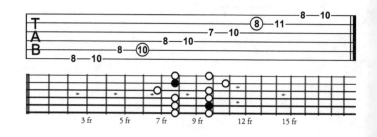

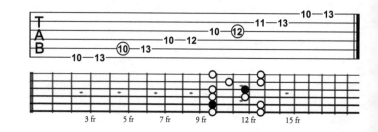

G

# G Blues

**SCALE DEGREES:** 1 ♭3 4 ♯4 5 ♭7
**SCALE TONES:** G B♭ C C♯ D F

This is a six-note scale and is really just a minor pentatonic with the addition of the ♯4.

Use this scale in the same places where you'd use the minor pentatonic, when you want a bluesy/rock effect.

This scale fits over the power chord (G5) as well as over a wide range of other chords in the minor and dominant categories. Try it over: Gm, Gm6, Gm7, Gm6/9, Gm(add9), Gm11, Gm7sus4, Gm13, G7, G9, and G7(♯9). It is even played over some major chords. Try it!

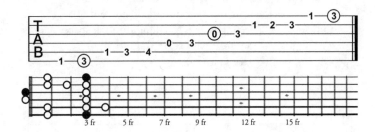

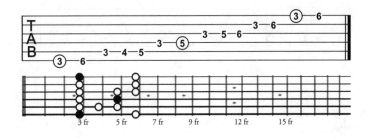

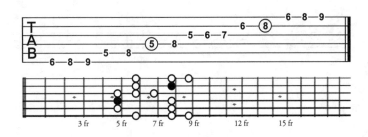

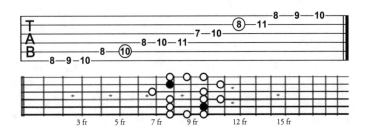

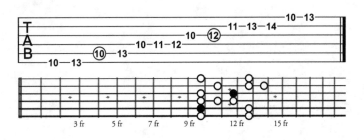

# G Whole Tone

**SCALE DEGREES:** 1 2 3 #4 #5 ♭7
**SCALE TONES:** G A B C# D# F

This six-note scale is probably the easiest to finger of any in this book. What makes it so simple is the fact that the distance from one note to the next is always the same, a whole-step. Because of this symmetry, any note in the scale can actually be called the root. The black dots in these patterns represent G notes, but feel free to start and end on any of the tones in the scale.

Only two fingerings are needed to play this scale since any fingering can be moved up or down the neck in two-fret increments.

The sound of this scale is unlike any other in this book due to the lack of half-steps. This lack of half-steps makes the scale feel very unsettled and void of a tonic note. The feeling is akin to falling through space.

This scale works great with G7(#5), G9(#5), G7(♭5), G9(♭5), G13(♭5), or G13(#5).

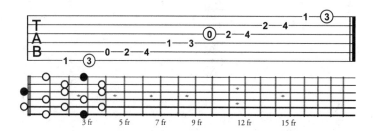

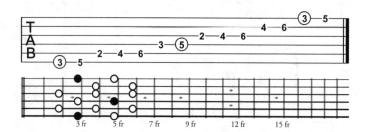

G

106

The GUITAR SCALE Picture Book

# G#/Ab

Scales and Modes

# G♯/A♭ Major

**SCALE DEGREES:** 1 2 3 4 5 6 7
**SCALE TONES:** A♭ B♭ C D♭ E♭ F G

The A♭ major scale (also known as Ionian) can be effectively played over many different A♭ major chords: A♭sus2, A♭6, A♭6/9, A♭maj7, A♭(add9) and A♭maj9. If you are going to use it to solo over the simpler A♭ major triad, then you'll want to avoid starting and stopping your solo on the 4th and 7th scale degrees. If you eliminate these two scale degrees from the major scale, you are left with the major pentatonic scale.

# G♯/A♭ Dorian

**SCALE DEGREES:** 1 2 ♭3 4 5 6 ♭7
**SCALE TONES:** A♭ B♭ C♭ D♭ E♭ F G♭

Dorian is the second mode of the major scale. So A♭ Dorian is the same as G♭ major, starting and ending on A♭.

The Dorian mode is a type of minor scale. It is often used when soloing over minor chords and sounds great when played over these chords: A♭m, A♭m6, A♭m6/9, A♭m9, A♭m7, A♭m(add9), A♭m11 and A♭m13. It is also possible to play it over a A♭5 (A♭ power chord). Even though the power chord isn't officially a chord at all, the A♭ Dorian mode will still sound cool over it.

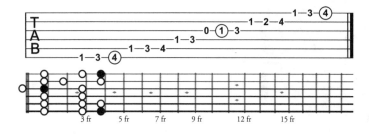

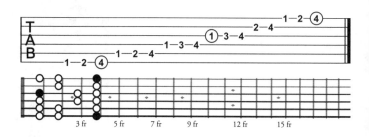

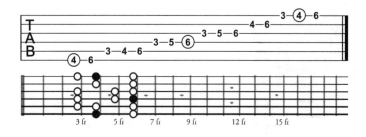

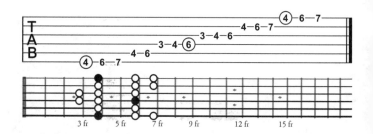

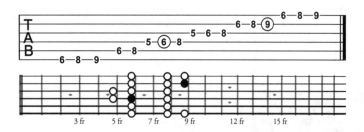

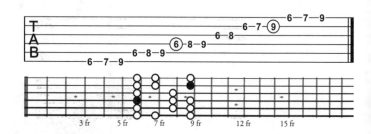

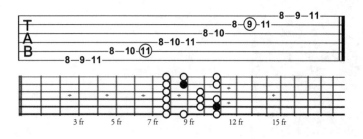

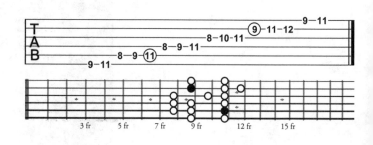

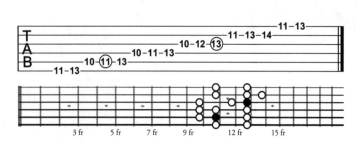

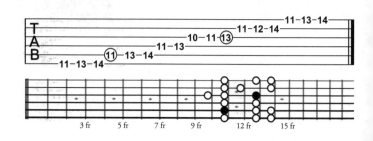

# G#/A♭ Phrygian

**SCALE DEGREES:** 1 ♭2 ♭3 4 5 ♭6 ♭7
**SCALE TONES:** G# A B C# D# E F#

Phrygian is the third mode of the major scale. So G#
Phrygian is the same as E major, starting and ending
on G#.

The sound is very distinctive due to the fact that it
begins with a half-step.

Sometimes called a "Spanish" or flamenco scale, its
sound is neither clearly major, minor, nor dominant. It
is possible to use it over a G#maj chord, but it is better
suited to G#sus, G#7sus, G#7sus(♭9). It also sounds
good played over the power chord (G#5).

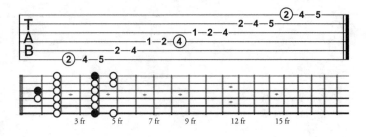

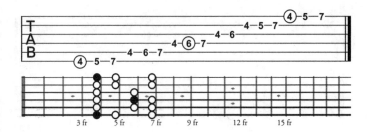

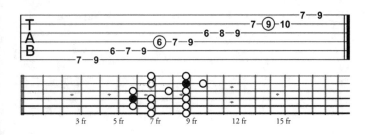

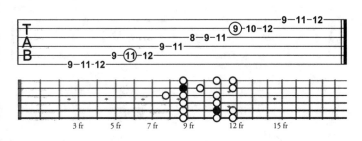

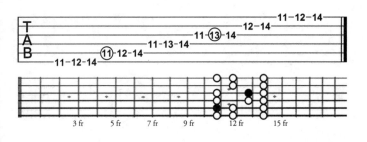

# G#/A♭ Lydian

**SCALE DEGREES:** 1 2 3 #4 5 6 7
**SCALE TONES:** A♭ B♭ C D E♭ F G

Lydian is the fourth mode of the major scale. So A♭ Lydian
is the same as E♭ major, starting and ending on A♭.

Lydian is the jazz musician's major scale. The inclusion
of the #4 imparts an urbane and sophisticated sound. The
personality of the scale is found in the 3rd, #4th and 7th
tones. Focus on these notes when playing this scale.

It will work over these chords: A♭maj, A♭6, A♭maj7(♭5),
A♭maj7(#11), A♭maj9(♭5), A♭maj9(#11), A♭6(♭5),
A♭6/9(♭5), and A♭6/9(#11). It will also work over the
power chord (A♭5).

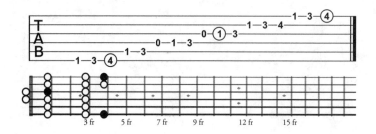

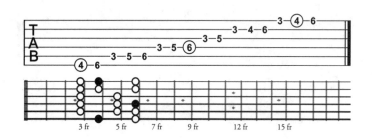

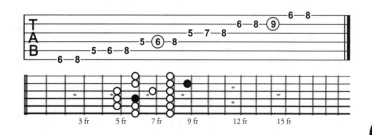

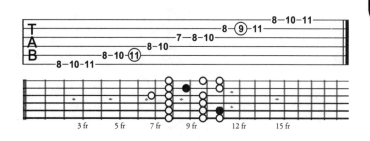

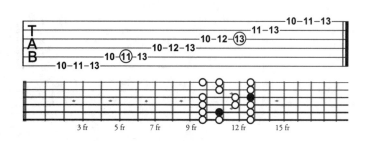

**G#**
**A♭**

# G#/A♭ Mixolydian

**SCALE DEGREES:** 1 2 3 4 5 6 ♭7
**SCALE TONES:** A♭ B♭ C D♭ E♭ F G♭

Mixolydian is the fifth mode of the major scale. So A♭ Mixolydian is the same as D♭ major, starting and ending on A♭.

The Mixolydian mode is a great blues, soul, R&B, and funk scale. It is often used alongside the blues scale when playing over unaltered dominant chords like: A♭7, A♭7sus, A♭9, A♭9sus, A♭11, A♭13, and A♭13sus. It will also work over the power chord (A♭5).

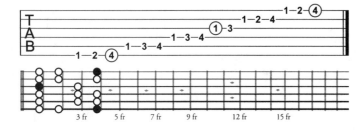

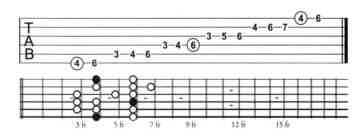

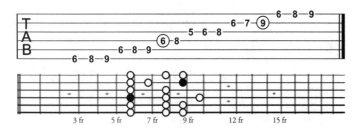

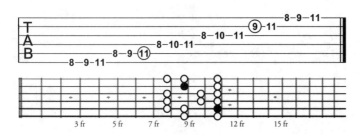

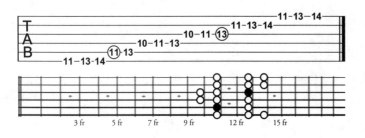

# G#/A♭ Aeolian

**SCALE DEGREES:** 1 2 ♭3 4 5 ♭6 ♭7
**SCALE TONES:** G# A# B C# D# E F#

Aeolian is the sixth mode of the major scale. So G# Aeolian is the same as B major, starting and ending on G#.

The Aeolian mode is known by several other names: pure minor, natural minor, and relative minor. With so many names you might think this is an important mode, and you'd be correct. This is the mode to use when improvising in minor key songs. It isn't the only scale choice for minor chords (see Dorian, harmonic minor, minor pentatonic and melodic/jazz minor).

In addition to the power chord (G#5), this mode will work over G#m, G#m(add9), G#m7, G#m7(#5), G#m9, and G#m(#5).

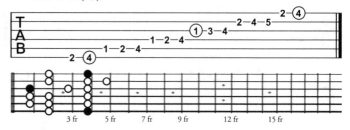

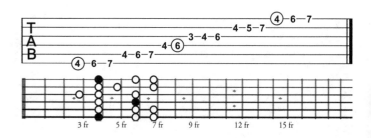

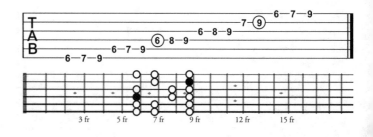

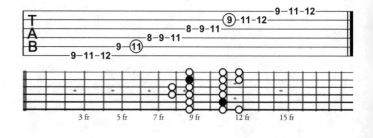

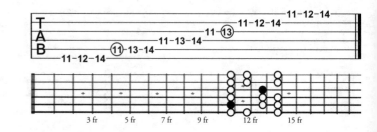

G#
A♭

# G#/A♭ Locrian

**SCALE DEGREES:**  1  ♭2  ♭3  4  ♭5  ♭6  ♭7
**SCALE TONES:**  G#  A  B  C#  D  E  F#

Locrian is the seventh mode of the major scale. So G#
Locrian is the same as A major, starting and ending
on G#.

The Locrian mode is the last mode derived from
the major scale. It is seldom used in contemporary
pop and rock music. Jazz musicians use it when
playing over min7(♭5) chords. It has many altered
tones, and as such, is unsuitable for use over most
other types of minor chords. Use it over G#m7(♭5).

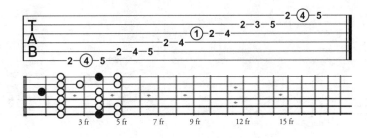

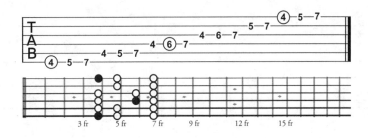

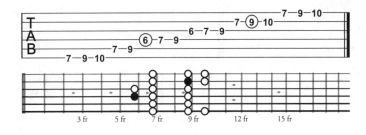

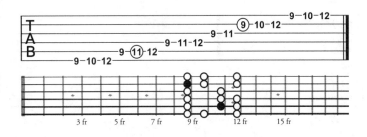

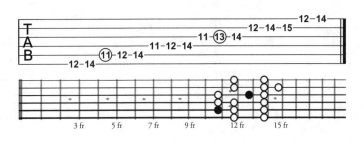

G#
A♭

111

# G#/A♭ Harmonic Minor

SCALE DEGREES: 1  2  ♭3  4  5  ♭6  7
SCALE TONES: A♭  B♭  C♭  D♭  E♭  F♭  G

In construction, this scale is very similar to the Aeolian mode. The only difference between the two is the 7th scale degree. The Aeolian has a lowered 7th.

Some people feel that this scale has a Middle Eastern flavor; others sense a Baroque connection. It is a sound adopted by some metal-style guitarists.

Use it over A♭m, A♭m(♯7), A♭m(maj7), A♭m(add9), A♭m7, A♭m9(maj7), and A♭m9(♮7). It will also work over the A♭ power chord (A♭5).

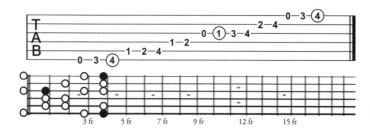

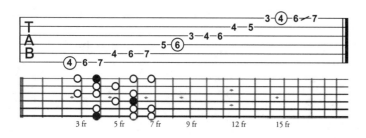

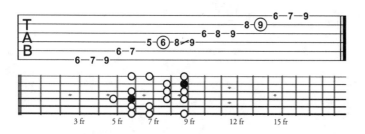

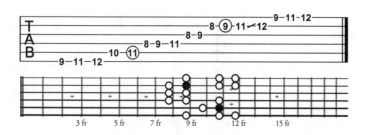

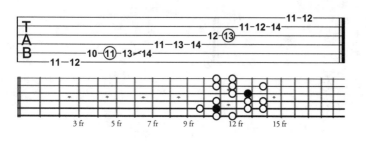

# G#/A♭ Phrygian Dominant

SCALE DEGREES: 1  ♭2  3  4  5  ♭6  ♭7
SCALE TONES: A♭  B♭♭  C  D♭  E♭  F♭  G♭

Phrygian Dominant is the fifth mode of the harmonic minor scale. So A♭ Phrygian Dominant is the same as D♭ harmonic minor.

It is a scale that is best suited for use when you want to add some tension tones over altered dominant 7th chords. It contains the ♯5 and ♭9 altered tones. These aren't tones you'd typically add to any major or minor chords. It is best suited for A♭7(♯5), A♭7(♭9), A♭13(♭9), and A♭7(♯5♭9).

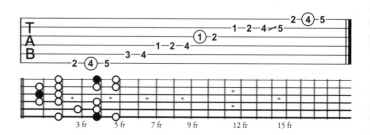

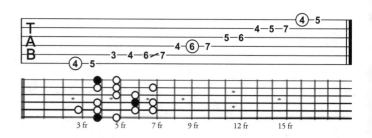

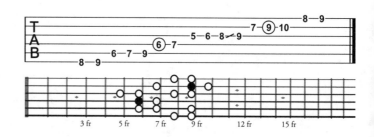

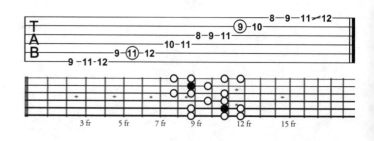

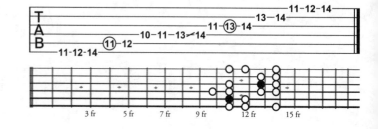

# G♯/A♭ Jazz Melodic Minor

SCALE DEGREES: 1 2 ♭3 4 5 6 7
SCALE TONES: A♭ B♭ C♭ D♭ E♭ F G

There are actually two forms of the melodic minor scale, an ascending form (same as the scale shown here) and a descending form (same notes as the Aeolian mode). For purposes of improvisation, only the ascending version of the scale is used. The term "jazz minor" is used to describe this ascending only version of the scale.

While it is possible to use it over a power chord (A♭5), this scale is most often played over: A♭m, A♭m(add9), A♭m6, A♭m6/9, A♭m(♯7), A♭m(maj7), A♭m(add9), A♭m6/9(♯7), and A♭m6/9(maj7).

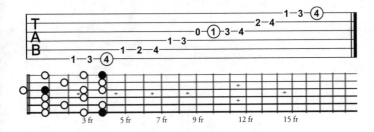

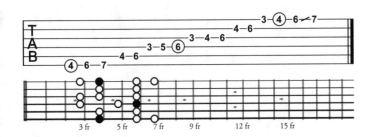

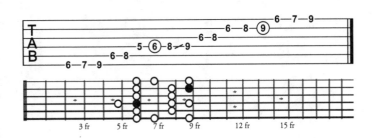

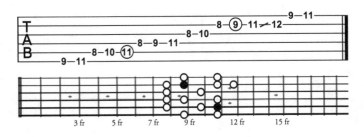

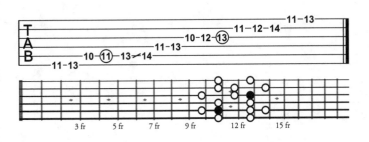

# G♯/A♭ Lydian Dominant

SCALE DEGREES: 1 2 3 ♯4 5 6 ♭7
SCALE TONES: A♭ B♭ C D E♭ F G♭

Lydian Dominant is the fourth mode of the melodic minor scale. So A♭ Lydian Dominant is the same as E♭ melodic minor played from A♭ to A♭.

Like some of the other scales, this mode goes by a couple of other names: Mixolydian ♯4 and Lydian ♭7. It isn't used as a minor scale by improvisers since it is better suited to dominant chords that contain a ♭5 or ♯11. It is very similar to both the Lydian and Mixolydian modes as the alternate names suggest.

While it is possible to use it over a power chord (A♭5), this scale is most often played over: A♭7, A♭7(♭5), A♭7(♯11), A♭9, A♭9(♭5), A♭9(♯11), A♭13(♯11), and A♭13(♭5).

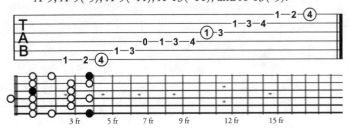

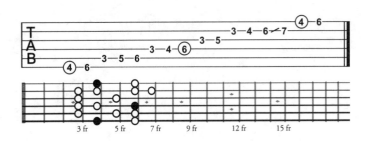

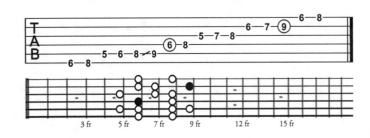

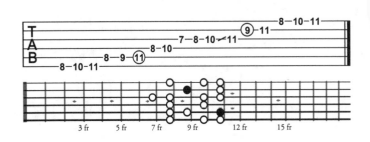

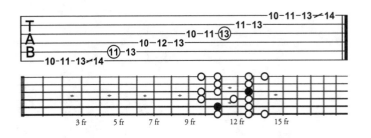

# G#/Ab Super Locrian

**SCALE DEGREES:** 1  b2  b3  b4  b5  b6  b7
**SCALE TONES:** G#  A  B  C  D  E  F#

Super Locrian is the seventh mode of the melodic minor scale. So G# Super Locrian is the same as A melodic minor played from G# to G#.

The "diminished/whole-tone scale," and "altered scale" are two alternate names for this mode.

This mode contains all of the tension tones that can be absorbed in a dominant chord. These tones are the b5, #5, b9, and #9.

Use it over G#7, G#7(b5), G#7(#5), G#7(b5b9), G#7(b5#9), G#7(#11), G#7(b9), G#7(#9), G#13(b9), and G#13(#9).

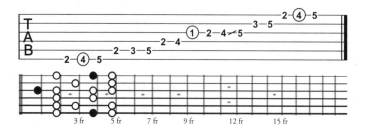

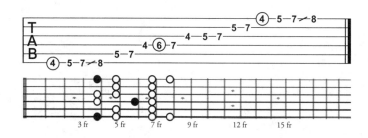

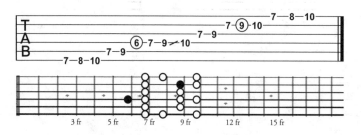

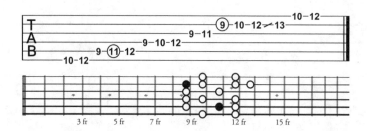

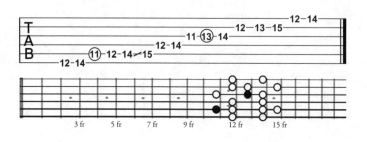

# G♯/A♭ Diminished (whole-half)

**SCALE DEGREES:** 1  2  ♭3  4  ♭5  ♯5  6  7
**SCALE TONES:** A♭  B♭  C♭  D♭  E♭♭  E  F  G

Sometimes called the symmetrical or fully diminished scale, this eight-note scale has some unusual traits. It is useful to understand how the scale is constructed. The primary notes of the scale are those that make up the diminished 7th chord: 1-♭3-♭5-♭♭7. The intervals that occur between these notes are all minor 3rds. The other four notes in this scale are located one half-step below each of these chord tones.

The symmetry in this scale lies in the basic building block of a whole-step followed by a half-step. This "cell" is repeated until the octave is reached.

This symmetry results in the fact that every third note can be considered the root note of the scale. The scale shown here will work with the A♭dim7, Bdim7, Ddim7, and Fdim7 chords. The grey notes in the scale patterns represent these alternate root tones. The scale can be started or ended on either the solid black notes or the grey notes.

Note that the scale pattern repeats itself every three frets, making it quite easy to play at any location on the fingerboard.

# G♯/A♭ Diminished (half-whole)

**SCALE DEGREES:** 1  ♭2  ♭3  ♮3  ♯4  5  6  ♭7
**SCALE TONES:** A♭  B♭♭  C♭  C♮  D  E♭  F  G♭

Like the diminished scale (whole-half), this scale is symmetrical. It is the only mode possible in the diminished scale and it is exactly the same as the whole-half diminished scale, except it begins with a half-step instead of a whole-step. The basic building block consists of a half-step followed by a whole-step. This sequence repeats until the octave is reached.

All of this symmetry results in the fact that every third note can be considered the root note of the scale. The scale shown here will work with the A♭7, A♭7(♭9), A♭7(♯9), A♭7(♭5), A♭7(♯11), A♭13(♭9), A♭7(♭5♭9), and A♭7(♭5♯9) chords. The only altered dominant chords that don't work with this scale are the ones that contain a ♯5.

The diminished scales are the only eight note scales in common use. Most scales have seven different notes.

The grey notes in the scale patterns represent alternate root tones. The scale can be started or ended on either the solid black notes or the grey notes.

Note that the scale pattern repeats itself every three frets, making it quite easy to play at any location on the fingerboard. Just transpose either of these patterns up or down the fingerboard a distance of three frets.

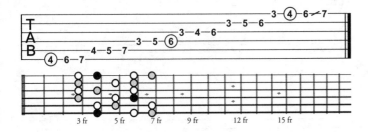

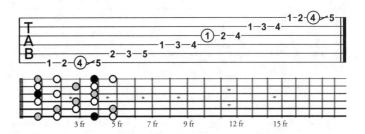

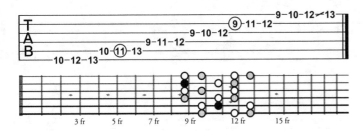

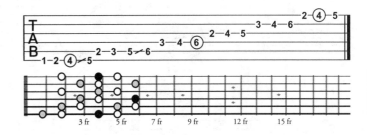

G♯/A♭

# G♯/A♭ Major Pentatonic

**SCALE DEGREES:** 1 2 3 5 6
**SCALE TONES:** A♭ B♭ C E♭ F

The major pentatonic scale only has five notes, but it is a scale that is very useful when working in folk, pop, country, and bluegrass styles. This scale avoids the possible dissonance contained in the standard major scale by eliminating the 4th and 7th scale degrees. It can be used over a power chord (A♭5) as well as A♭maj, A♭6, A♭6/9, A♭(add9), A♭sus2, A♭maj7 and A♭maj9.

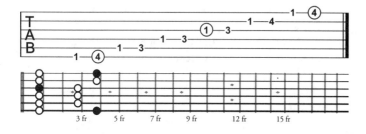

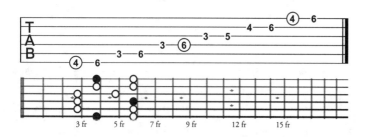

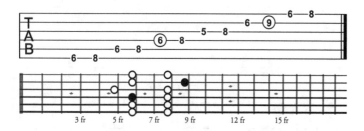

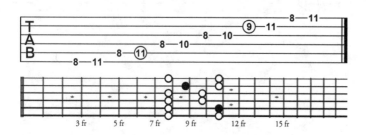

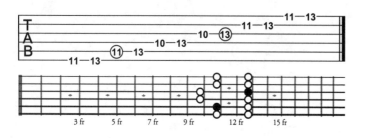

# G♯/A♭ Minor Pentatonic

**SCALE DEGREES:** 1 ♭3 4 5 ♭7
**SCALE TONES:** A♭ C♭ D♭ E♭ G♭

Like the major pentatonic, this scale only contains five notes and is often called the rock scale. It can be traced to the Aeolian (natural minor scale) with two notes removed, the 2nd and 6th.

This scale fits over the power chord (A♭5) as well as over A♭m, A♭m6, A♭m7, A♭m6/9, A♭m(add9), A♭m11, A♭m7sus4, A♭m13, A♭7, A♭9, and A♭7(♯9). In general, use it when you want a rock sound, even if the chord is major.

Since this scale is very similar to the blues scale, they may be used in place of each other.

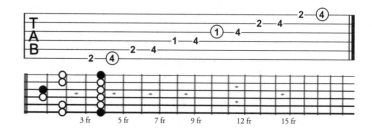

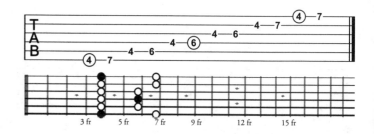

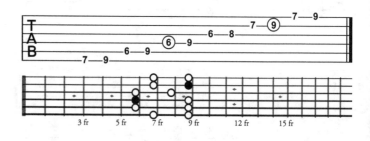

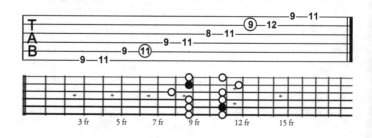

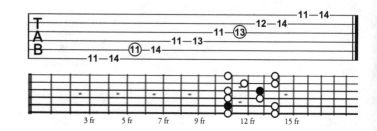

G♯
A♭

# G#/A♭ Blues

**SCALE DEGREES:** 1  ♭3  4  #4  5  ♭7
**SCALE TONES:** A♭  C♭  D♭  D♮  E♭  G♭

This is a six-note scale and is really just a minor pentatonic with the addition of the #4.

Use this scale in the same places where you'd use the minor pentatonic, when you want a bluesy/rock effect.

This scale fits over the power chord (A♭5) as well as over a wide range of other chords in the minor and dominant categories. Try it over: A♭m, A♭m6, A♭m7, A♭m6/9, A♭m(add9), A♭m11, A♭m7sus4, A♭m13, A♭7, A♭9, and A♭7(#9). It is even played over some major chords. Try it!

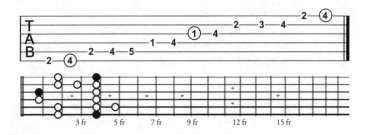

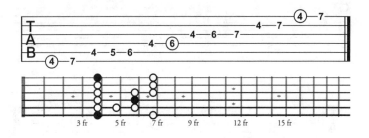

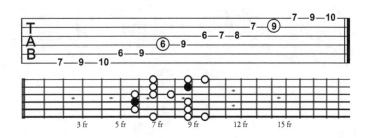

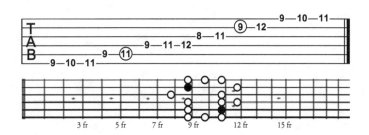

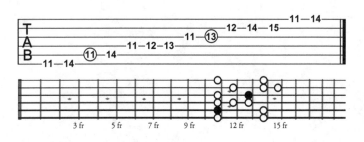

117

# G#/A♭ Whole Tone

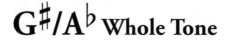

**SCALE DEGREES:** 1  2  3  #4  #5  ♭7
**SCALE TONES:** A♭  B♭  C  D  E  G♭

This six-note scale is probably the easiest to finger of any in this book. What makes it so simple is the fact that the distance from one note to the next is always the same, a whole-step. Because of this symmetry, any note in the scale can actually be called the root. The black dots in these patterns represent A♭ notes, but feel free to start and end on any of the tones in the scale.

Only two fingerings are needed to play this scale since any fingering can be moved up or down the neck in two-fret increments.

The sound of this scale is unlike any other in this book due to the lack of half-steps. This lack of half-steps makes the scale feel very unsettled and void of a tonic note. The feeling is akin to falling through space.

This scale works great with A♭7(#5), A♭9(#5), A♭7(♭5), A♭9(♭5), A♭13(♭5), or A♭13(#5).

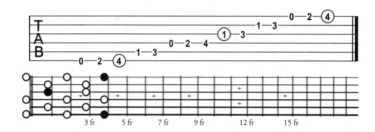

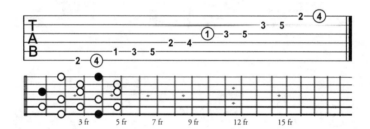

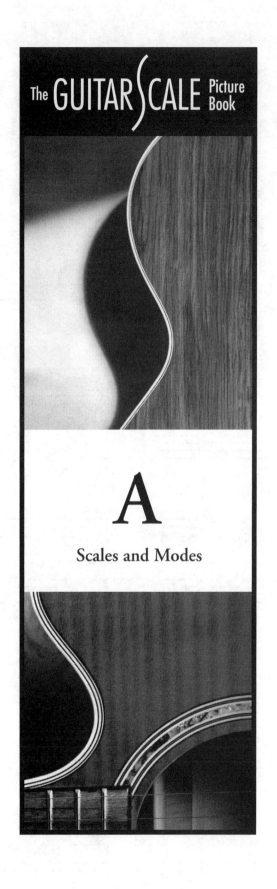

The GUITAR SCALE Picture Book

# A

### Scales and Modes

# A Major

**SCALE DEGREES:** 1 2 3 4 5 6 7
**SCALE TONES:** A B C# D E F# G#

The A major scale (also known as Ionian) can be effectively played over many different A major chords: Asus2, A6, A6/9, Amaj7, A(add9) and Amaj9. If you are going to use it to solo over the simpler A major triad, then you'll want to avoid starting and stopping your solo on the 4th and 7th scale degrees. If you eliminate these two scale degrees from the major scale, you are left with the major pentatonic scale.

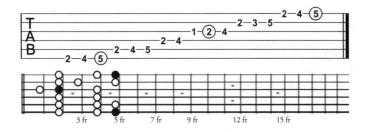

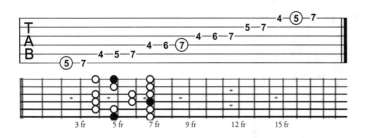

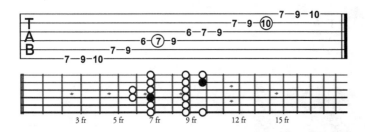

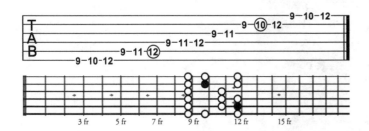

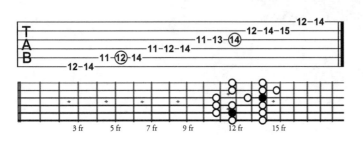

# A Dorian

**SCALE DEGREES:** 1 2 ♭3 4 5 6 ♭7
**SCALE TONES:** A B C D E F# G

Dorian is the second mode of the major scale. So A Dorian is the same as G major, starting and ending on A.

The Dorian mode is a type of minor scale. It is often used when soloing over minor chords and sounds great when played over these chords: Am, Am6, Am6/9, Am9, Am7, Am(add9), Am11 and Am13. It is also possible to play it over a A5 (A power chord). Even though the power chord isn't officially a chord at all, the A Dorian mode will still sound cool over it.

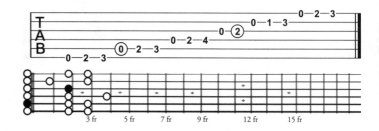

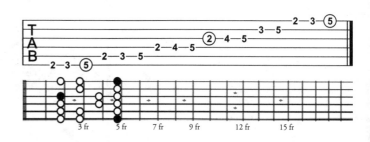

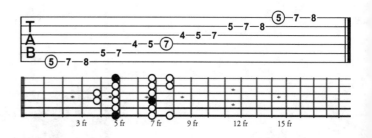

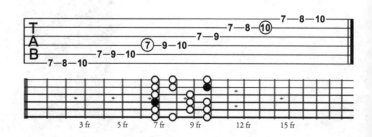

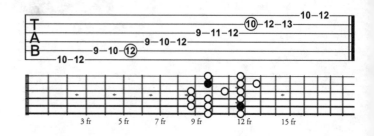

# A Phrygian

**SCALE DEGREES:** 1 ♭2 ♭3 4 5 ♭6 ♭7
**SCALE TONES:** A B♭ C D E F G

Phrygian is the third mode of the major scale. So A Phrygian is the same as F major, starting and ending on A.

The sound is very distinctive due to the fact that it begins with a half-step.

Sometimes called a "Spanish" or flamenco scale, its sound is neither clearly major, minor, nor dominant. It is possible to use it over a Amaj chord, but it is better suited to Asus, A7sus, A7sus(♭9). It also sounds good played over the power chord (A5).

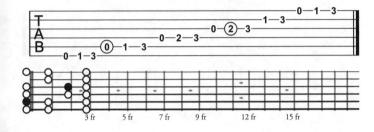

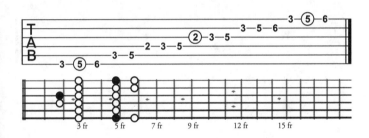

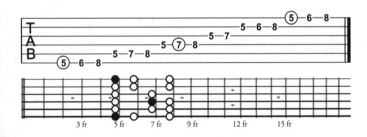

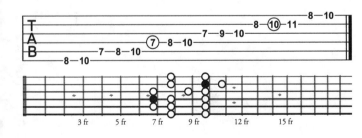

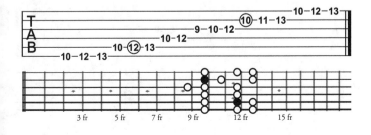

# A Lydian

**SCALE DEGREES:** 1 2 3 ♯4 5 6 7
**SCALE TONES:** A B C♯ D♯ E F♯ G♯

Lydian is the fourth mode of the major scale. So A Lydian is the same as E major, starting and ending on A.

Lydian is the jazz musician's major scale. The inclusion of the ♯4 imparts an urbane and sophisticated sound. The personality of the scale is found in the 3rd, ♯4th and 7th tones. Focus on these notes when playing this scale.

It will work over these chords: Amaj, A6, Amaj7(♭5), Amaj7(♯11), Amaj9(♭5), Amaj9(♯11), A6(♭5), A6/9(♭5), and A6/9(♯11). It will also work over the power chord (A5).

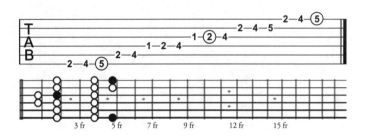

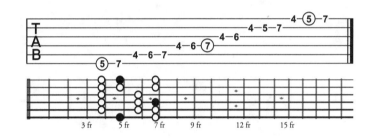

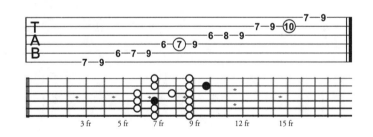

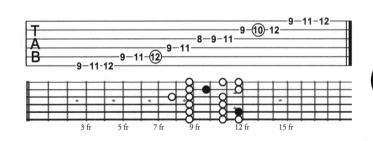

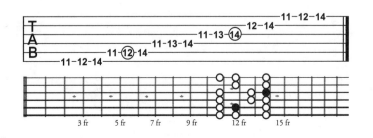

A

# A Mixolydian

**SCALE DEGREES:** 1 2 3 4 5 6 ♭7
**SCALE TONES:** A B C♯ D E F♯ G

Mixolydian is the fifth mode of the major scale. So A Mixolydian is the same as D major, starting and ending on A.

The Mixolydian mode is a great blues, soul, R&B, and funk scale. It is often used alongside the blues scale when playing over unaltered dominant chords like: A7, A7sus, A9, A9sus, A11, A13, and A13sus. It will also work over the power chord (A5).

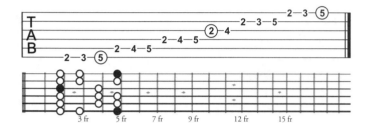

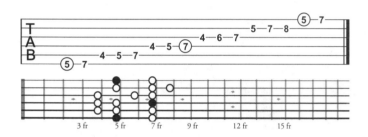

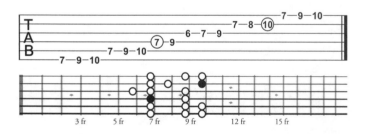

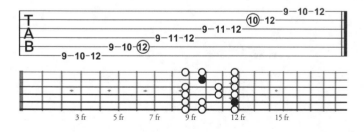

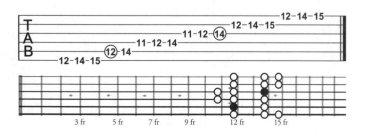

# A Aeolian

**SCALE DEGREES:** 1 2 ♭3 4 5 ♭6 ♭7
**SCALE TONES:** A B C D E F G

Aeolian is the sixth mode of the major scale. So A Aeolian is the same as C major, starting and ending on A.

The Aeolian mode is known by several other names: pure minor, natural minor, and relative minor. With so many names you might think this is an important mode, and you'd be correct. This is the mode to use when improvising in minor key songs. It isn't the only scale choice for minor chords (see Dorian, harmonic minor, minor pentatonic and melodic/jazz minor).

In addition to the power chord (A5), this mode will work over Am, Am(add9), Am7, Am7(♯5), Am9, and Am(♯5).

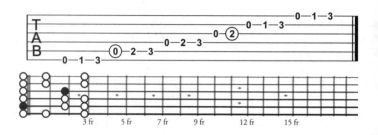

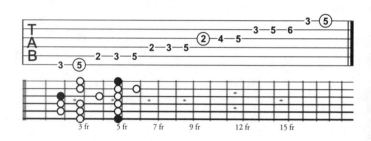

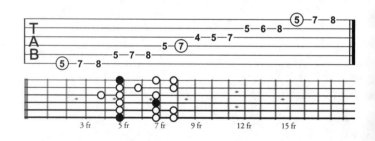

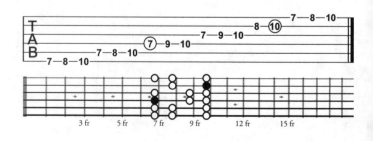

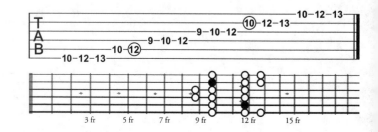

# A Locrian

**SCALE DEGREES:** 1 ♭2 ♭3 4 ♭5 ♭6 ♭7
**SCALE TONES:** A B♭ C D E♭ F G

Locrian is the seventh mode of the major scale. So A Locrian is the same as B♭ major, starting and ending on A.

The Locrian mode is the last mode derived from the major scale. It is seldom used in contemporary pop and rock music. Jazz musicians use it when playing over min7(♭5) chords. It has many altered tones, and as such, is unsuitable for use over most other types of minor chords. Use it over Am7(♭5).

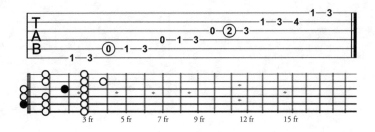

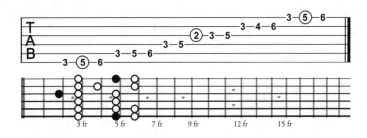

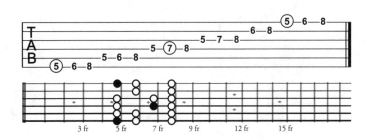

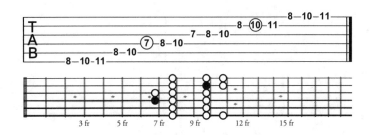

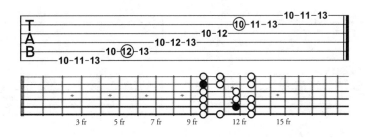

# A Harmonic Minor

**SCALE DEGREES:** 1 2 ♭3 4 5 ♭6 7
**SCALE TONES:** A B C D E F G♯

In construction, this scale is very similar to the Aeolian mode. The only difference between the two is the 7th scale degree. The Aeolian has a lowered 7th.

Some people feel that this scale has a Middle Eastern flavor; others sense a Baroque connection. It is a sound adopted by some metal-style guitarists.

Use it over Am, Am(♯7), Am(maj7), Am(add9), Am7, Am9(maj7), and Am9(♮7). It will also work over the A power chord (A5).

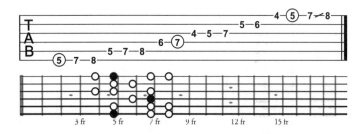

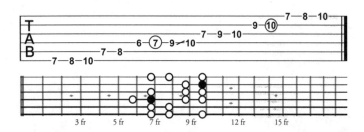

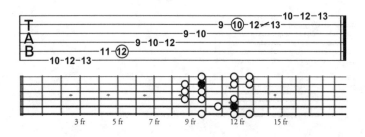

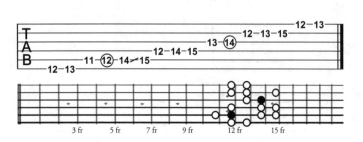

# A Phrygian Dominant

**SCALE DEGREES:** 1 ♭2 3 4 5 ♭6 ♭7
**SCALE TONES:** A B♭ C♯ D E F G

Phrygian Dominant is the fifth mode of the harmonic minor scale. So A Phrygian Dominant is the same as D harmonic minor.

It is a scale that is best suited for use when you want to add some tension tones over altered dominant 7th chords. It contains the ♯5 and ♭9 altered tones. These aren't tones you'd typically add to any major or minor chords. It is best suited for A7(♯5), A7(♭9), A13(♭9), and A7(♯5♭9).

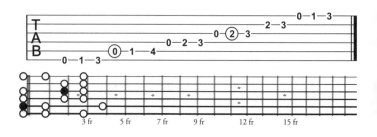

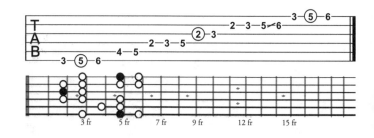

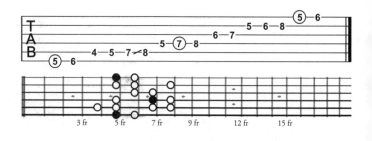

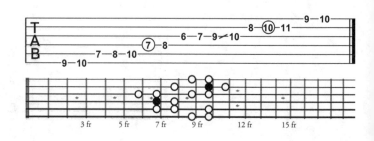

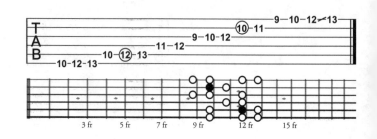

# A Jazz Melodic Minor

SCALE DEGREES: 1 2 ♭3 4 5 6 7
SCALE TONES: A B C D E F♯ G♯

There are actually two forms of the melodic minor scale, an ascending form (same as the scale shown here) and a descending form (same notes as the Aeolian mode). For purposes of improvisation, only the ascending version of the scale is used. The term "jazz minor" is used to describe this ascending only version of the scale.

While it is possible to use it over a power chord (A5), this scale is most often played over: Am, Am(add9), Am6, Am6/9, Am(♯7), Am(maj7), Am(add9), Am6/9(♯7), and Am6/9(maj7).

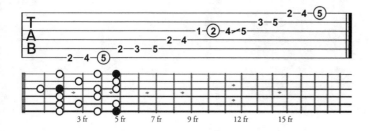

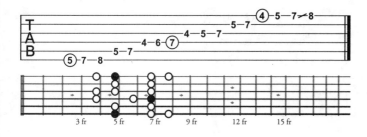

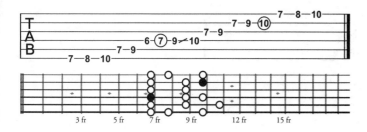

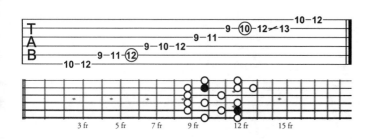

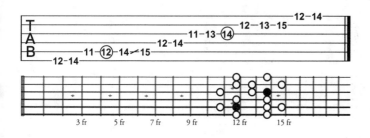

# A Lydian Dominant

SCALE DEGREES: 1 2 3 ♯4 5 6 ♭7
SCALE TONES: A B C♯ D♯ E ♯F G

Lydian Dominant is the fourth mode of the melodic minor scale. So A Lydian Dominant is the same as E melodic minor played from A to A.

Like some of the other scales, this mode goes by a couple of other names: Mixolydian ♯4 and Lydian ♭7. It isn't used as a minor scale by improvisers since it is better suited to dominant chords that contain a ♭5 or ♯11. It is very similar to both the Lydian and Mixolydian modes as the alternate names suggest.

While it is possible to use it over a power chord (A5), this scale is most often played over: A7, A7(♭5), A7(♯11), A9, A9(♭5), A9(♯11), A13(♯11), and A13(♭5).

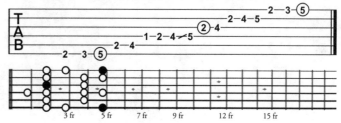

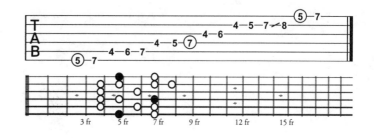

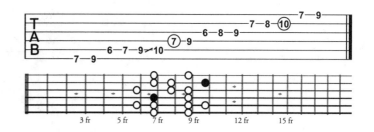

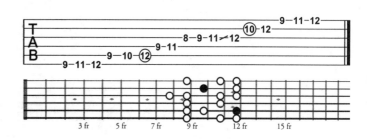

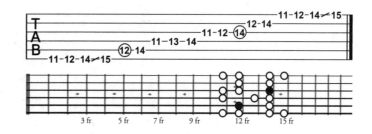

# A Super Locrian

SCALE DEGREES:  1  ♭2  ♭3  ♭4  ♭5  ♭6  ♭7
SCALE TONES:  A  B♭  C  D♭  E♭  F  G

Super Locrian is the seventh mode of the melodic minor scale. So A Super Locrian is the same as B♭ melodic minor played from A to A.

The "diminished/whole-tone scale," and "altered scale" are two alternate names for this mode.

This mode contains all of the tension tones that can be absorbed in a dominant chord. These tones are the ♭5, ♯5, ♭9, and ♯9.

Use it over A7, A7(♭5), A7(♯5), A7(♭5♭9), A7(♭5♯9), A7(♯11), A7(♭9), A7(♯9), A13(♭9), and A13(♯9).

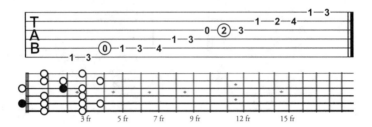

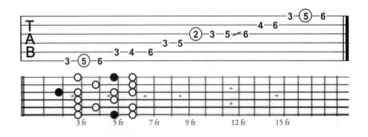

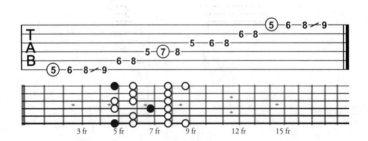

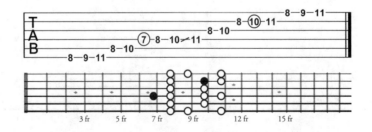

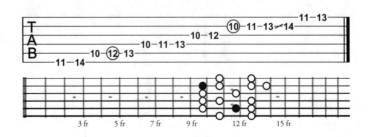

# A Diminished (whole-half)

**SCALE DEGREES:** 1 2 ♭3 4 ♭5 ♯5 6 7
**SCALE TONES:** A B C D E♭ E♯ F♯ G♯

Sometimes called the symmetrical or fully diminished scale, this eight-note scale has some unusual traits. It is useful to understand how the scale is constructed. The primary notes of the scale are those that make up the diminished 7th chord: 1-♭3-♭5-♭♭7. The intervals that occur between these notes are all minor 3rds. The other four notes in this scale are located one half-step below each of these chord tones.

The symmetry in this scale lies in the basic building block of a whole-step followed by a half-step. This "cell" is repeated until the octave is reached.

This symmetry results in the fact that every third note can be considered the root note of the scale. The scale shown here will work with the Cdim7, E♭dim7, G♭dim7, and Adim7 chords. The grey notes in the scale patterns represent these alternate root tones. The scale can be started or ended on either the solid black notes or the grey notes.

Note that the scale pattern repeats itself every three frets, making it quite easy to play at any location on the fingerboard.

# A Diminished (half-whole)

**SCALE DEGREES:** 1 ♭2 ♭3 ♮3 ♯4 5 6 ♭7
**SCALE TONES:** A B♭ C C♯ D♯ E F♯ G

Like the diminished scale (whole-half), this scale is symmetrical. It is the only mode possible in the diminished scale and it is exactly the same as the whole-half diminished scale, except it begins with a half-step instead of a whole-step. The basic building block consists of a half-step followed by a whole-step. This sequence repeats until the octave is reached.

All of this symmetry results in the fact that every third note can be considered the root note of the scale. The scale shown here will work with the A7, A7(♭9), A7(♯9), A7(♭5), A7(♯11), A13(♭9), A7(♭5♭9), and A7(♭5♯9) chords. The only altered dominant chords that don't work with this scale are the ones that contain a ♯5.

The diminished scales are the only eight note scales in common use. Most scales have seven different notes.

The grey notes in the scale patterns represent alternate root tones. The scale can be started or ended on either the solid black notes or the grey notes.

Note that the scale pattern repeats itself every three frets, making it quite easy to play at any location on the fingerboard. Just transpose either of these patterns up or down the fingerboard a distance of three frets.

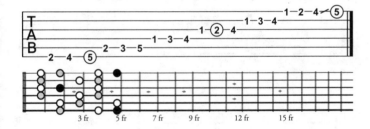

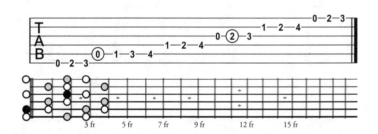

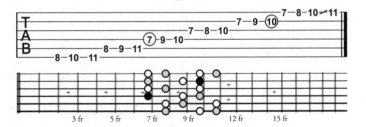

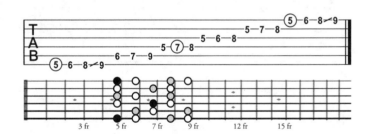

A

# A Major Pentatonic

**SCALE DEGREES:** 1 2 3 5 6
**SCALE TONES:** A B C♯ E F♯

The major pentatonic scale only has five notes, but it is a scale that is very useful when working in folk, pop, country, and bluegrass styles. This scale avoids the possible dissonance contained in the standard major scale by eliminating the 4th and 7th scale degrees. It can be used over a power chord (A5) as well as Amaj, A6, A6/9, A(add9), Asus2, Amaj7 and Amaj9.

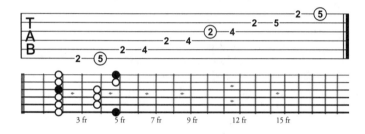

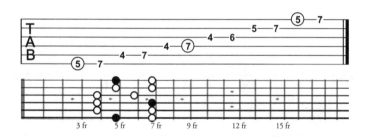

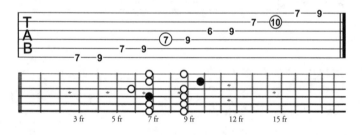

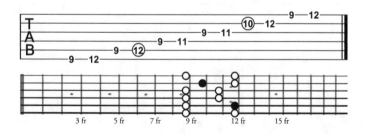

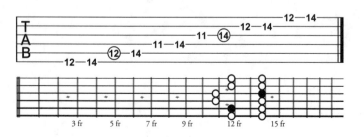

# A Minor Pentatonic

**SCALE DEGREES:** 1 ♭3 4 5 ♭7
**SCALE TONES:** A C D E G

Like the major pentatonic, this scale only contains five notes and is often called the rock scale. It can be traced to the Aeolian (natural minor scale) with two notes removed, the 2nd and 6th.

This scale fits over the power chord (A5) as well as over Am, Am6, Am7, Am6/9, Am(add9), Am11, Am7sus4, Am13, A7, A9, and A7(♯9). In general, use it when you want a rock sound, even if the chord is major.

Since this scale is very similar to the blues scale, they may be used in place of each other.

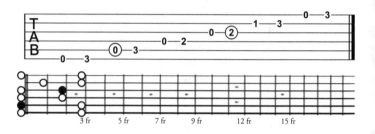

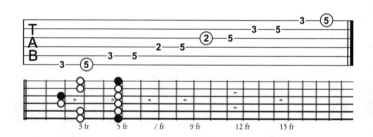

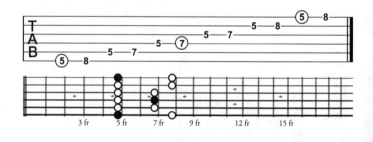

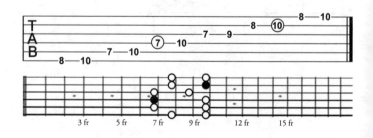

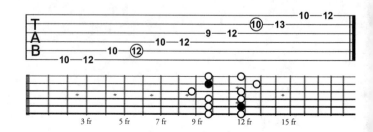

A

# A Blues

**SCALE DEGREES:** 1 ♭3 4 ♯4 5 ♭7
**SCALE TONES:** A C D D♯ E G

This is a six-note scale and is really just a minor pentatonic with the addition of the ♯4.

Use this scale in the same places where you'd use the minor pentatonic, when you want a bluesy/rock effect.

This scale fits over the power chord (A5) as well as over a wide range of other chords in the minor and dominant categories. Try it over: Am, Am6, Am7, Am6/9, Am(add9), Am11, Am7sus4, Am13, A7, A9, and A7(♯9). It is even played over some major chords. Try it!

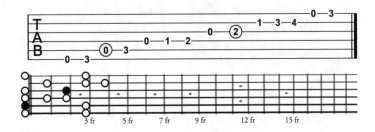

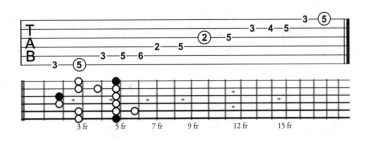

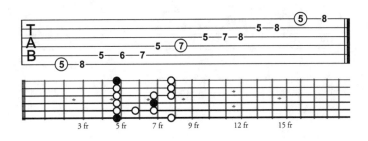

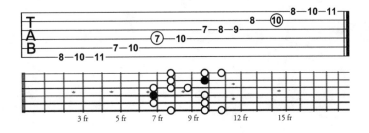

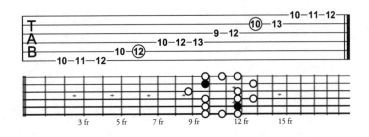

# A Whole Tone

**SCALE DEGREES:** 1  2  3  #4  #5  b7
**SCALE TONES:**  A  B  C#  D#  E#  G

This six-note scale is probably the easiest to finger of any in this book. What makes it so simple is the fact that the distance from one note to the next is always the same, a whole-step. Because of this symmetry, any note in the scale can actually be called the root. The black dots in these patterns represent A notes, but feel free to start and end on any of the tones in the scale.

Only two fingerings are needed to play this scale since any fingering can be moved up or down the neck in two-fret increments.

The sound of this scale is unlike any other in this book due to the lack of half-steps. This lack of half-steps makes the scale feel very unsettled and void of a tonic note. The feeling is akin to falling through space.

This scale works great with A7(#5), A9(#5), A7(b5), A9(b5), A13(b5), or A13(#5).

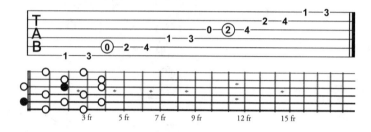

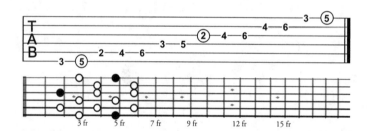

A

130

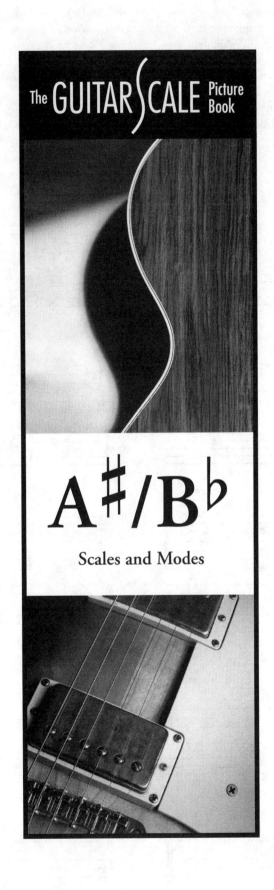

# The GUITAR SCALE Picture Book

## A♯/B♭

### Scales and Modes

# A#/B♭ Major

**SCALE DEGREES:** 1 2 3 4 5 6 7
**SCALE TONES:** B♭ C D E♭ F G A

The B♭ major scale (also known as Ionian) can be effectively played over many different B♭ major chords: B♭sus2, B♭6, B♭6/9, B♭maj7, B♭(add9) and B♭maj9. If you are going to use it to solo over the simpler B♭ major triad, then you'll want to avoid starting and stopping your solo on the 4th and 7th scale degrees. If you eliminate these two scale degrees from the major scale, you are left with the major pentatonic scale.

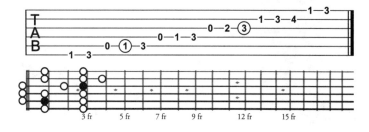

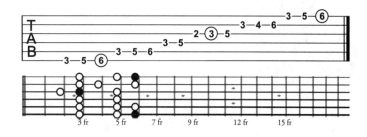

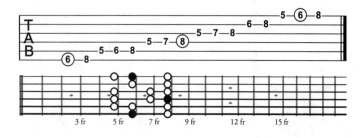

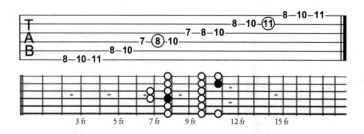

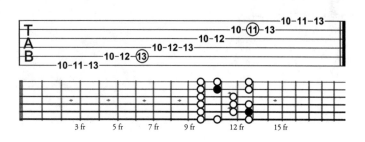

# A#/B♭ Dorian

**SCALE DEGREES:** 1 2 ♭3 4 5 6 ♭7
**SCALE TONES:** B♭ C D♭ E♭ F G A♭

Dorian is the second mode of the major scale. So B♭ Dorian is the same as A♭ major, starting and ending on B♭.

The Dorian mode is a type of minor scale. It is often used when soloing over minor chords and sounds great when played over these chords: B♭m, B♭m6, B♭m6/9, B♭m9, B♭m7, B♭m(add9), B♭m11 and B♭m13. It is also possible to play it over a B♭5 (B♭ power chord). Even though the power chord isn't officially a chord at all, the B♭ Dorian mode will still sound cool over it.

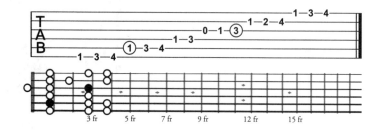

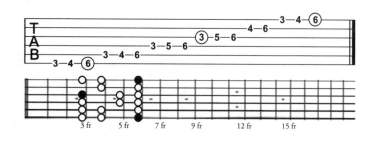

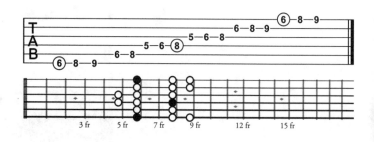

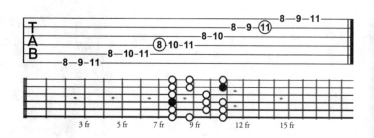

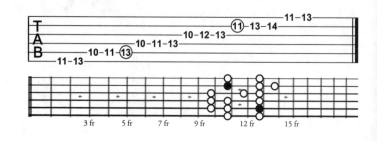

A#
B♭

132

# A♯/B♭ Phrygian

**SCALE DEGREES:** 1 ♭2 ♭3 4 5 ♭6 ♭7
**SCALE TONES:** B♭ C♭ D♭ E♭ F G♭ A♭

Phrygian is the third mode of the major scale. So B♭ Phrygian is the same as G♭ major, starting and ending on B♭.

The sound is very distinctive due to the fact that it begins with a half-step.

Sometimes called a "Spanish" or flamenco scale, its sound is neither clearly major, minor, nor dominant. It is possible to use it over a B♭maj chord, but it is better suited to B♭sus, B♭7sus, B♭7sus(♭9). It also sounds good played over the power chord (B♭5).

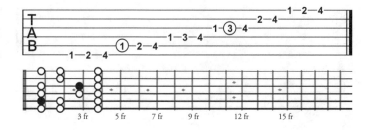

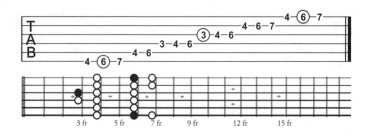

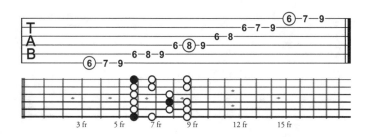

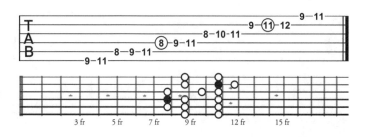

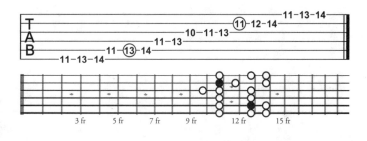

# A♯/B♭ Lydian

**SCALE DEGREES:** 1 2 3 ♯4 5 6 7
**SCALE TONES:** B♭ C D E F G A

Lydian is the fourth mode of the major scale. So B♭ Lydian is the same as F major, starting and ending on B♭.

Lydian is the jazz musician's major scale. The inclusion of the ♯4 imparts an urbane and sophisticated sound. The personality of the scale is found in the 3rd, ♯4th and 7th tones. Focus on these notes when playing this scale.

It will work over these chords: B♭maj, B♭6, B♭maj7(♭5), B♭maj7(♯11), B♭maj9(♭5), B♭maj9(♯11), B♭6(♭5), B♭6/9(♭5), and B♭6/9(♯11). It will also work over the power chord (B♭5).

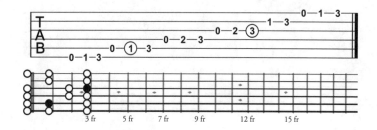

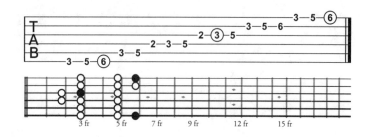

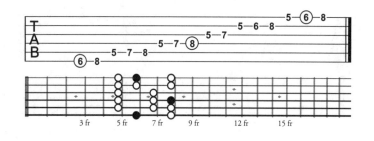

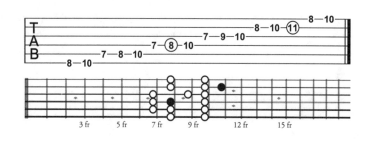

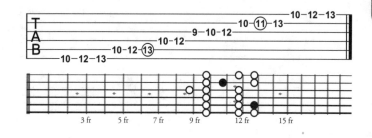

A♯
B♭

133

# A♯/B♭ Mixolydian

SCALE DEGREES: 1 2 3 4 5 6 ♭7
SCALE TONES: B♭ C D E♭ F G A♭

Mixolydian is the fifth mode of the major scale. So B♭ Mixolydian is the same as E♭ major, starting and ending on B♭.

The Mixolydian mode is a great blues, soul, R&B, and funk scale. It is often used alongside the blues scale when playing over unaltered dominant chords like: B♭7, B♭7sus, B♭9, B♭9sus, B♭11, B♭13, and B♭13sus. It will also work over the power chord (B♭5).

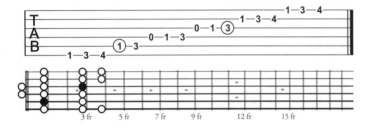

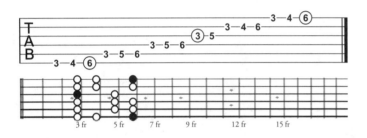

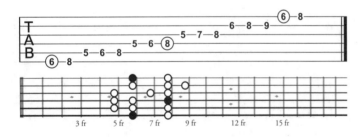

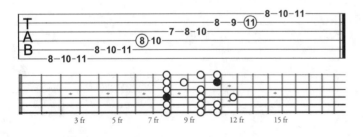

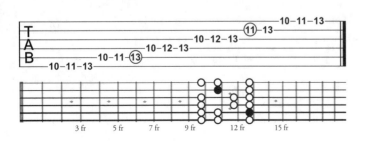

# A♯/B♭ Aeolian

SCALE DEGREES: 1 2 ♭3 4 5 ♭6 ♭7
SCALE TONES: B♭ C D♭ E♭ F G♭ A♭

Aeolian is the sixth mode of the major scale. So B♭ Aeolian is the same as D♭ major, starting and ending on B♭.

The Aeolian mode is known by several other names: pure minor, natural minor, and relative minor. With so many names you might think this is an important mode, and you'd be correct. This is the mode to use when improvising in minor key songs. It isn't the only scale choice for minor chords (see Dorian, harmonic minor, minor pentatonic and melodic/jazz minor).

In addition to the power chord (B♭5), this mode will work over B♭m, B♭m(add9), B♭m7, B♭m7(♯5), B♭m9, and B♭m(♯5).

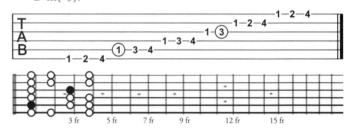

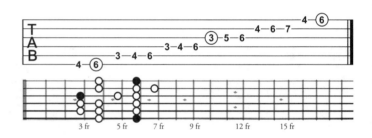

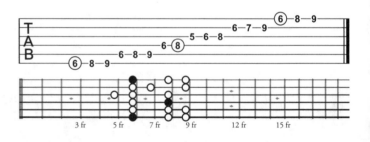

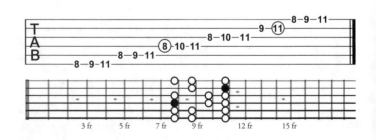

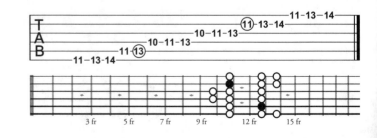

A♯
B♭

# A#/B♭ Locrian

**SCALE DEGREES:** 1 ♭2 ♭3 4 ♭5 ♭6 ♭7
**SCALE TONES:** A# B C# D# E F# G#

Locrian is the seventh mode of the major scale. So A#
Locrian is the same as B major, starting and ending on A#.

The Locrian mode is the last mode derived from the
major scale. It is seldom used in contemporary pop and
rock music. Jazz musicians use it when playing over
min7(♭5) chords. It has many altered tones, and as such, is
unsuitable for use over most other types of minor chords.
Use it over A#m7(♭5) and B♭m7(♭5).

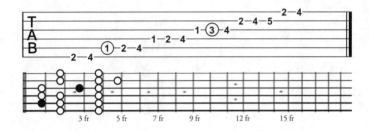

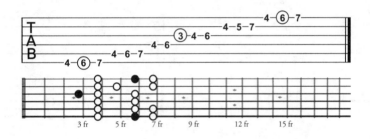

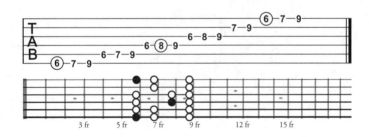

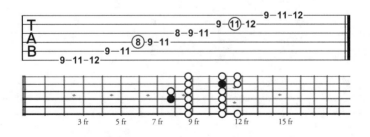

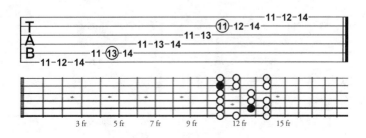

135

# A#/B♭ Harmonic Minor

SCALE DEGREES: 1 2 ♭3 4 5 ♭6 7
SCALE TONES: B♭ C D♭ E♭ F G♭ A

In construction, this scale is very similar to the Aeolian mode. The only difference between the two is the 7th scale degree. The Aeolian has a lowered 7th.

Some people feel that this scale has a Middle Eastern flavor; others sense a Baroque connection. It is a sound adopted by some metal-style guitarists.

Use it over B♭m, B♭m(♯7), B♭m(maj7), B♭m(add9), B♭m7, B♭m9(maj7), and B♭m9(♮7). It will also work over the B♭ power chord (B♭5).

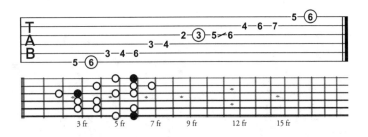

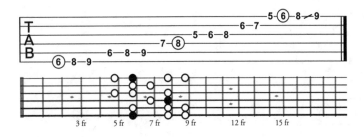

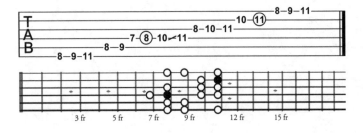

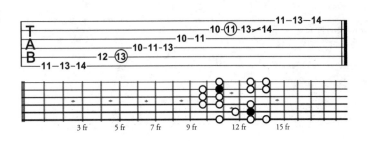

# A#/B♭ Phrygian Dominant

SCALE DEGREES: 1 ♭2 3 4 5 ♭6 ♭7
SCALE TONES: B♭ C♭ D E♭ F G♭ A♭

Phrygian Dominant is the fifth mode of the harmonic minor scale. So B♭ Phrygian Dominant is the same as E♭ harmonic minor.

It is a scale that is best suited for use when you want to add some tension tones over altered dominant 7th chords. It contains the ♯5 and ♭9 altered tones. These aren't tones you'd typically add to any major or minor chords. It is best suited for B♭7(♯5), B♭7(♭9), B♭13(♭9), and B♭7(♯5♭9).

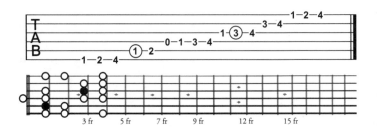

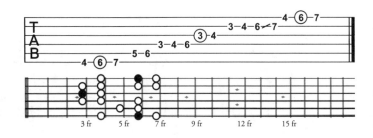

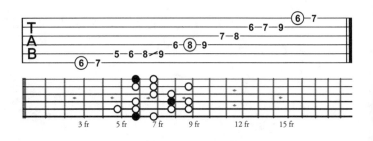

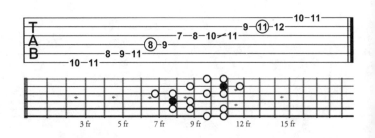

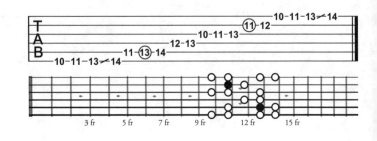

# A#/B♭ Jazz Melodic Minor

**SCALE DEGREES:** 1 2 ♭3 4 5 6 7
**SCALE TONES:** B♭ C D♭ E♭ F G A

There are actually two forms of the melodic minor scale, an ascending form (same as the scale shown here) and a descending form (same notes as the Aeolian mode). For purposes of improvisation, only the ascending version of the scale is used. The term "jazz minor" is used to describe this ascending only version of the scale.

While it is possible to use it over a power chord (B♭5), this scale is most often played over: B♭m, B♭m(add9), B♭m6, B♭m6/9, B♭m(♯7), B♭m(maj7), B♭m(add9), B♭m6/9(♯7), and B♭m6/9(maj7).

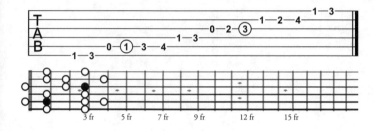

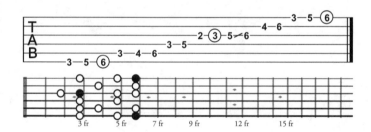

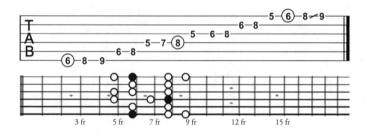

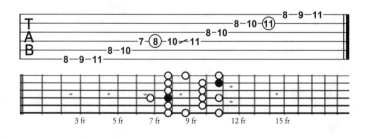

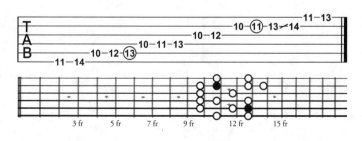

# A#/B♭ Lydian Dominant

**SCALE DEGREES:** 1 2 3 ♯4 5 6 ♭7
**SCALE TONES:** B♭ C D E F G A♭

Lydian Dominant is the fourth mode of the melodic minor scale. So B♭ Lydian Dominant is the same as F melodic minor played from B♭ to B♭.

Like some of the other scales, this mode goes by a couple of other names: Mixolydian ♯4 and Lydian ♭7. It isn't used as a minor scale by improvisers since it is better suited to dominant chords that contain a ♭5 or ♯11. It is very similar to both the Lydian and Mixolydian modes as the alternate names suggest.

While it is possible to use it over a power chord (B♭5), this scale is most often played over: B♭7, B♭7(♭5), B♭7(♯11), B♭9, B♭9(♭5), B♭9(♯11), B♭13(♯11), and B♭13(♭5).

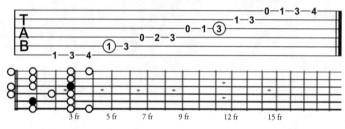

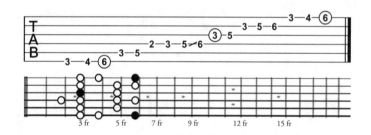

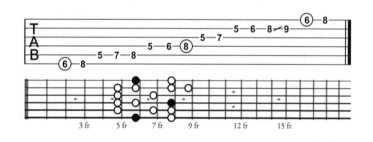

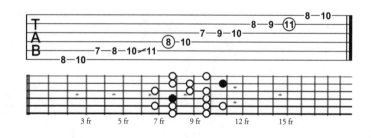

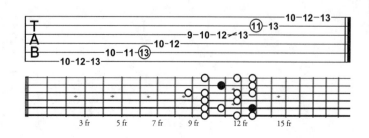

A#
B♭

137

# A♯/B♭ Super Locrian

**SCALE DEGREES:** 1 ♭2 ♭3 ♭4 ♭5 ♭6 ♭7
**SCALE TONES:** A♯ B C♯ D E F♯ G♯

Super Locrian is the seventh mode of the melodic minor scale. So A♯ Super Locrian is the same as B melodic minor played from A♯ to A♯.

The "diminished/whole-tone scale," and "altered scale" are two alternate names for this mode.

This mode contains all of the tension tones that can be absorbed in a dominant chord. These tones are the ♭5, ♯5, ♭9, and ♯9.

Use it over A♯7, A♯7(♭5), A♯7(♯5), A♯7(♭5♭9), A♯7(♭5♯9), A♯7(♯11), A♯7(♭9), A♯7(♯9), A♯13(♭9), and A♯13(♯9).

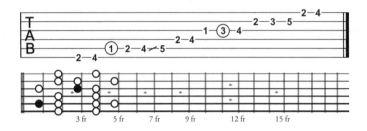

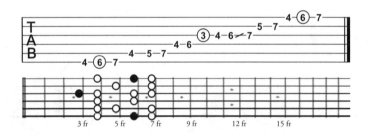

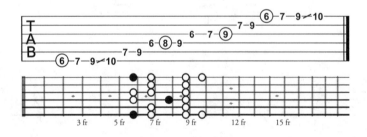

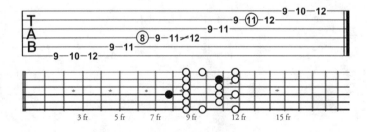

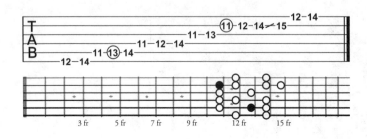

# A#/B♭ Diminished (whole-half)

**SCALE DEGREES:** 1  2  ♭3  4  ♭5  #5  6  7
**SCALE TONES:** B♭  C  D♭  E♭  F♭  F#  G  A

Sometimes called the symmetrical or fully diminished scale, this eight-note scale has some unusual traits. It is useful to understand how the scale is constructed. The primary notes of the scale are those that make up the diminished 7th chord: 1-♭3-♭5-♭♭7. The intervals that occur between these notes are all minor 3rds. The other four notes in this scale are located one half-step below each of these chord tones.

The symmetry in this scale lies in the basic building block of a whole-step followed by a half-step. This "cell" is repeated until the octave is reached.

This symmetry results in the fact that every third note can be considered the root note of the scale. The scale shown here will work with the B♭dim7, D♭dim7, Edim7, and Gdim7 chords. The grey notes in the scale patterns represent these alternate root tones. The scale can be started or ended on either the solid black notes or the grey notes.

Note that the scale pattern repeats itself every three frets, making it quite easy to play at any location on the fingerboard.

# A#/B♭ Diminished (half-whole)

**SCALE DEGREES:** 1  ♭2  ♭3  ♮3  #4  5  6  ♭7
**SCALE TONES:** B♭  C♭  D♭  D♮  E  F  G  A♭

Like the diminished scale (whole-half), this scale is symmetrical. It is the only mode possible in the diminished scale and it is exactly the same as the whole-half diminished scale, except it begins with a half-step instead of a whole-step. The basic building block consists of a half-step followed by a whole-step. This sequence repeats until the octave is reached.

All of this symmetry results in the fact that every third note can be considered the root note of the scale. The scale shown here will work with the B♭7, B♭7(♭9), B♭7(#9), B♭7(♭5), B♭7(#11), B♭13(♭9), B♭7(♭5♭9), and B♭7(♭5#9) chords. The only altered dominant chords that don't work with this scale are the ones that contain a #5.

The diminished scales are the only eight note scales in common use. Most scales have seven different notes.

The grey notes in the scale patterns represent alternate root tones. The scale can be started or ended on either the solid black notes or the grey notes.

Note that the scale pattern repeats itself every three frets, making it quite easy to play at any location on the fingerboard. Just transpose either of these patterns up or down the fingerboard a distance of three frets.

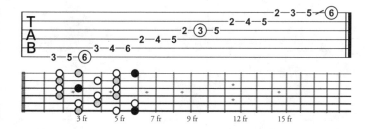

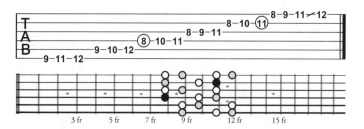

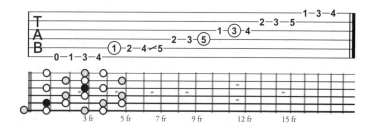

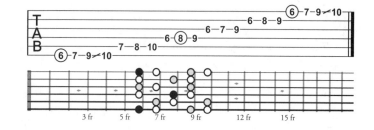

# A♯/B♭ Major Pentatonic

**SCALE DEGREES:** 1 2 3 5 6
**SCALE TONES:** B♭ C D F G

The major pentatonic scale only has five notes, but it is a scale that is very useful when working in folk, pop, country, and bluegrass styles. This scale avoids the possible dissonance contained in the standard major scale by eliminating the 4th and 7th scale degrees. It can be used over a power chord (B♭5) as well as B♭maj, B♭6, B♭6/9, B♭(add9), B♭sus2, B♭maj7 and B♭maj9.

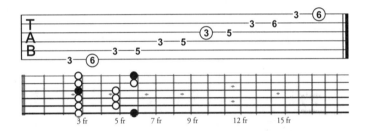

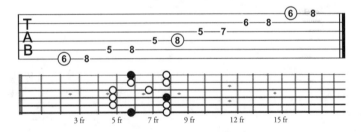

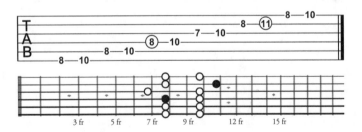

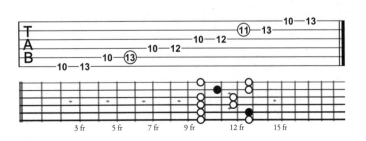

# A♯/B♭ Minor Pentatonic

**SCALE DEGREES:** 1 ♭3 4 5 ♭7
**SCALE TONES:** B♭ D♭ E♭ F A♭

Like the major pentatonic, this scale only contains five notes and is often called the rock scale. It can be traced to the Aeolian (natural minor scale) with two notes removed, the 2nd and 6th.

This scale fits over the power chord (B♭5) as well as over B♭m, B♭m6, B♭m7, B♭m6/9, B♭m(add9), B♭m11, B♭m7sus4, B♭m13, B♭7, B♭9, and B♭7(♯9). In general, use it when you want a rock sound, even if the chord is major.

Since this scale is very similar to the blues scale, they may be used in place of each other.

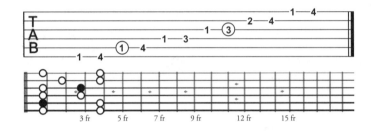

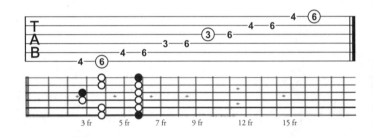

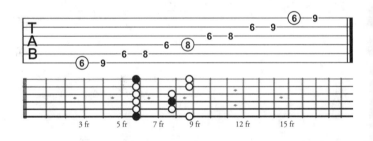

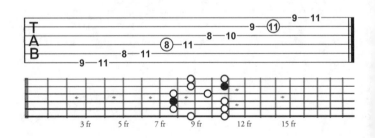

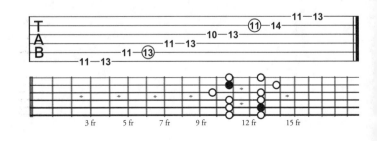

A♯
B♭

# A♯/B♭ Blues

**SCALE DEGREES:** 1  ♭3  4  ♯4  5  ♭7
**SCALE TONES:** B♭  D♭  E♭  E♮  F  A♭

This is a six-note scale and is really just a minor pentatonic with the addition of the ♯4.

Use this scale in the same places where you'd use the minor pentatonic, when you want a bluesy/rock effect.

This scale fits over the power chord (B♭5) as well as over a wide range of other chords in the minor and dominant categories. Try it over: B♭m, B♭m6, B♭m7, B♭m6/9, B♭m(add9), B♭m11, B♭m7sus4, B♭m13, B♭7, B♭9, and B♭7(♯9). It is even played over some major chords. Try it!

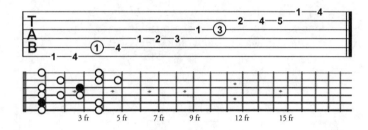

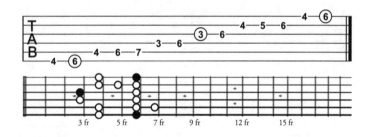

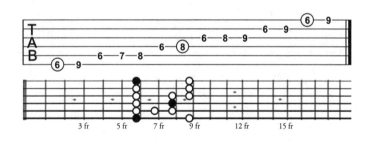

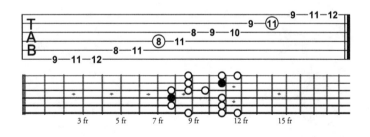

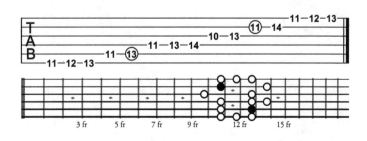

# A#/Bb Whole Tone

**SCALE DEGREES:** 1  2  3  #4  #5  b7
**SCALE TONES:** Bb  C  D  E  F#  Ab

This six-note scale is probably the easiest to finger of any in this book. What makes it so simple is the fact that the distance from one note to the next is always the same, a whole-step. Because of this symmetry, any note in the scale can actually be called the root. The black dots in these patterns represent Bb notes, but feel free to start and end on any of the tones in the scale.

Only two fingerings are needed to play this scale since any fingering can be moved up or down the neck in two-fret increments.

The sound of this scale is unlike any other in this book due to the lack of half-steps. This lack of half-steps makes the scale feel very unsettled and void of a tonic note. The feeling is akin to falling through space.

This scale works great with Bb7(#5), Bb9(#5), Bb7(b5), Bb9(b5), Bb13(b5), or Bb13(#5).

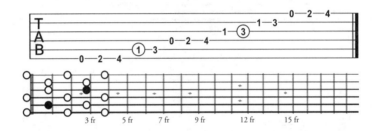

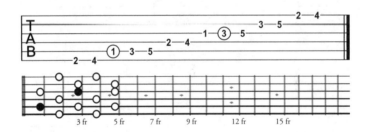

A#
Bb

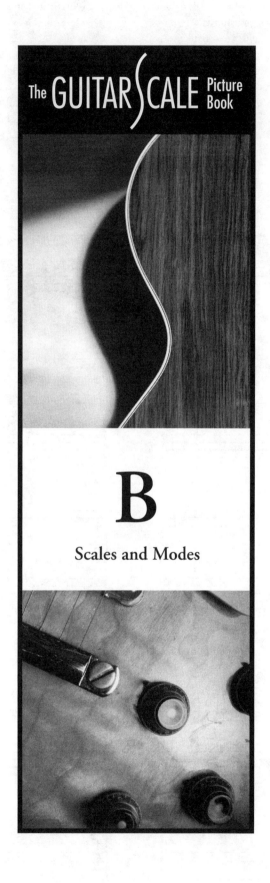

The GUITAR SCALE Picture Book

# B

### Scales and Modes

# B Major

**SCALE DEGREES:** 1 2 3 4 5 6 7
**SCALE TONES:** B C# D# E F# G# A#

The B major scale (also known as Ionian) can be
effectively played over many different B major chords:
Bsus2, B6, B6/9, Bmaj7, B(add9) and Bmaj9. If you are
going to use it to solo over the simpler B major triad,
then you'll want to avoid starting and stopping your
solo on the 4th and 7th scale degrees. If you eliminate
these two scale degrees from the major scale, you are left
with the major pentatonic scale.

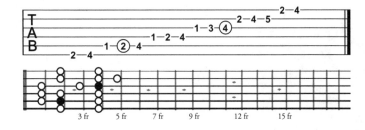

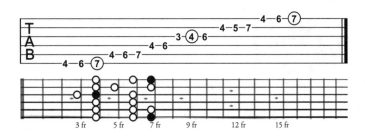

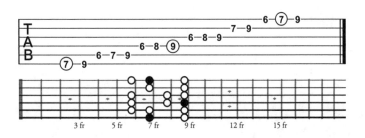

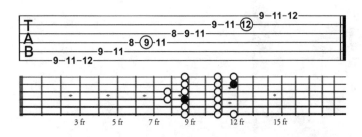

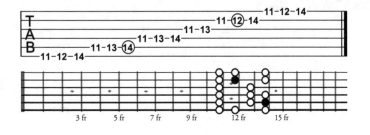

# B Dorian

**SCALE DEGREES:** 1 2 ♭3 4 5 6 ♭7
**SCALE TONES:** B C# D E F# G# A

Dorian is the second mode of the major scale. So B
Dorian is the same as A major, starting and ending
on B.

The Dorian mode is a type of minor scale. It is
often used when soloing over minor chords and
sounds great when played over these chords: Bm,
Bm6, Bm6/9, Bm9, Bm7, Bm(add9), Bm11 and
Bm13. It is also possible to play it over a B5 (B
power chord). Even though the power chord isn't
officially a chord at all, the B Dorian mode will still
sound cool over it.

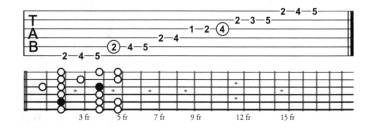

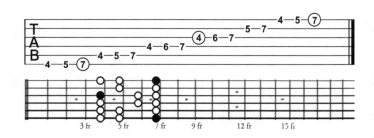

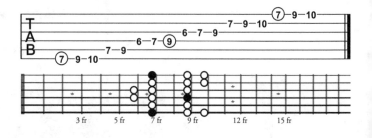

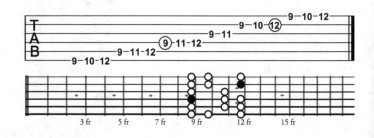

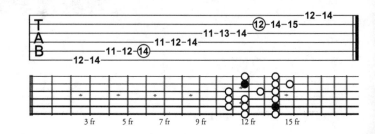

# B Phrygian

**SCALE DEGREES:** 1 ♭2 ♭3 4 5 ♭6 ♭7
**SCALE TONES:** B C D E F♯ G A

Phrygian is the third mode of the major scale. So B Phrygian is the same as G major, starting and ending on B.

The sound is very distinctive due to the fact that it begins with a half-step.

Sometimes called a "Spanish" or flamenco scale, its sound is neither clearly major, minor, nor dominant. It is possible to use it over a Bmaj chord, but it is better suited to Bsus, B7sus, B7sus(♭9). It also sounds good played over the power chord (B5).

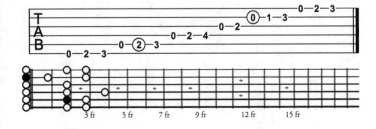

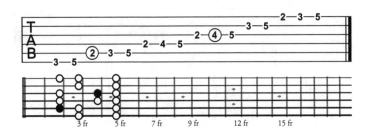

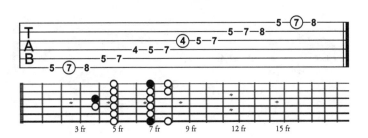

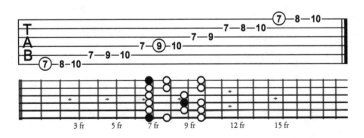

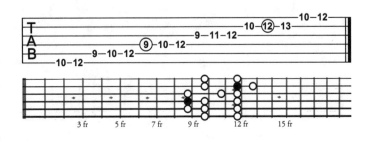

# B Lydian

**SCALE DEGREES:** 1 2 3 ♯4 5 6 7
**SCALE TONES:** B C♯ D♯ E♯ F♯ G♯ A♯

Lydian is the fourth mode of the major scale. So B Lydian is the same as F♯ major, starting and ending on B.

Lydian is the jazz musician's major scale. The inclusion of the ♯4 imparts an urbane and sophisticated sound. The personality of the scale is found in the 3rd, ♯4th and 7th tones. Focus on these notes when playing this scale.

It will work over these chords: Bmaj, B6, Bmaj7(♭5), Bmaj7(♯11), Bmaj9(♭5), Bmaj9(♯11), B6(♭5), C6/9(♭5), and B6/9(♯11). It will also work over the power chord (B5).

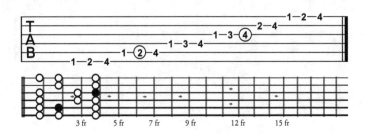

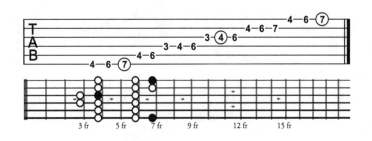

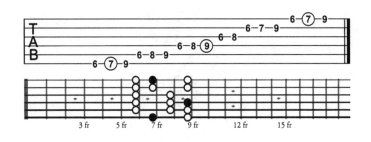

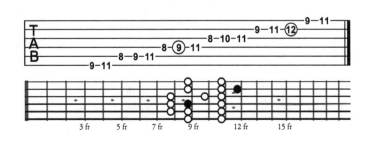

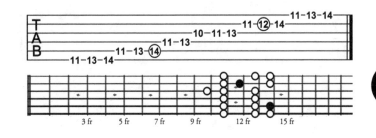

145

# B Mixolydian

**SCALE DEGREES:** 1   2   3   4   5   6   ♭7
**SCALE TONES:** B   C♯   D♯   E   F♯   G♯   A

Mixolydian is the fifth mode of the major scale. So B Mixolydian is the same as E major, starting and ending on B.

The Mixolydian mode is a great blues, soul, R&B, and funk scale. It is often used alongside the blues scale when playing over unaltered dominant chords like: B7, B7sus, B9, B9sus, B11, B13, and B13sus. It will also work over the power chord (B5).

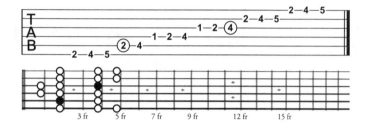

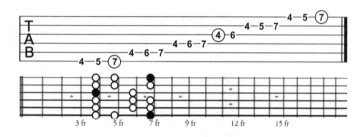

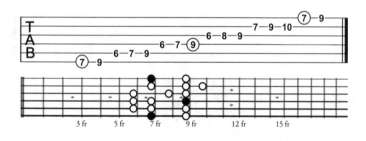

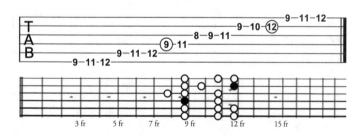

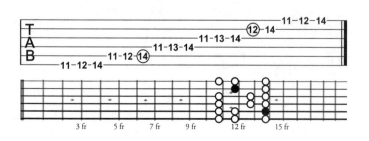

# B Aeolian

**SCALE DEGREES:** 1   2   ♭3   4   5   ♭6   ♭7
**SCALE TONES:** B   C♯   D   E   F♯   G   A

Aeolian is the sixth mode of the major scale. So B Aeolian is the same as D major, starting and ending on B.

The Aeolian mode is known by several other names: pure minor, natural minor, and relative minor. With so many names you might think this is an important mode, and you'd be correct. This is the mode to use when improvising in minor key songs. It isn't the only scale choice for minor chords (see Dorian, harmonic minor, minor pentatonic and melodic/jazz minor).

In addition to the power chord (B5), this mode will work over Bm, Bm(add9), Bm7, Bm7(♯5), Bm9, and Bm(♯5).

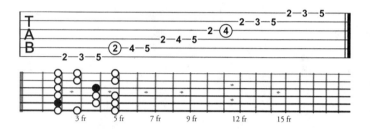

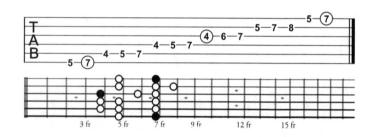

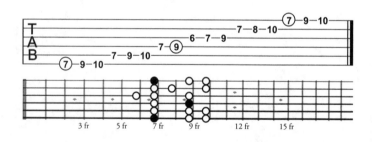

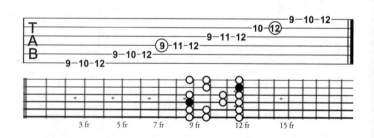

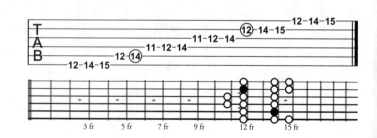

# B Locrian

**SCALE DEGREES:** 1 ♭2 ♭3 4 ♭5 ♭6 ♭7
**SCALE TONES:** B C D E F G A

Locrian is the seventh mode of the major scale. So B Locrian is the same as C major, starting and ending on B.

The Locrian mode is the last mode derived from the major scale. It is seldom used in contemporary pop and rock music. Jazz musicians use it when playing over min7(♭5) chords. It has many altered tones, and as such, is unsuitable for use over most other types of minor chords. Use it over Bm7(♭5).

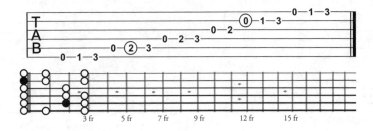

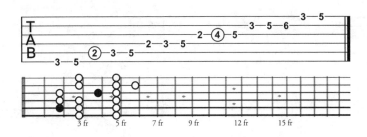

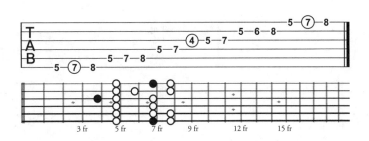

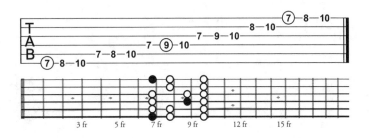

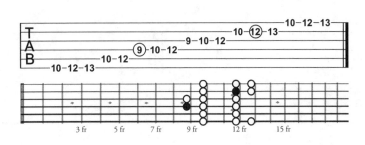

# B Harmonic Minor

**SCALE DEGREES:** 1  2  ♭3  4  5  ♭6  7
**SCALE TONES:** B  C#  D  E  F#  G  A#

In construction, this scale is very similar to the Aeolian mode. The only difference between the two is the 7th scale degree. The Aeolian has a lowered 7th.

Some people feel that this scale has a Middle Eastern flavor; others sense a Baroque connection. It is a sound adopted by some metal-style guitarists.

Use it over Bm, Bm(#7), Bm(maj7), Bm(add9), Bm7, Bm9(maj7), and Bm9(♭7). It will also work over the B power chord (B5).

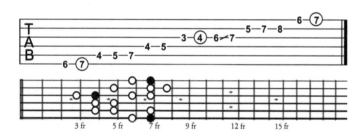

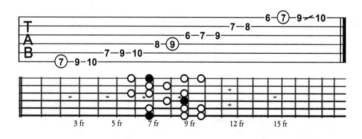

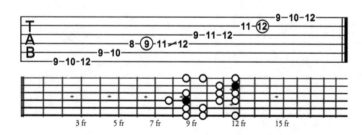

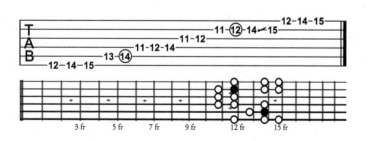

# B Phrygian Dominant

**SCALE DEGREES:** 1  ♭2  3  4  5  ♭6  ♭7
**SCALE TONES:** B  C  D#  E  F#  G  A

Phrygian Dominant is the fifth mode of the harmonic minor scale. So B Phrygian Dominant is the same as E harmonic minor.

It is a scale that is best suited for use when you want to add some tension tones over altered dominant 7th chords. It contains the #5 and ♭9 altered tones. These aren't tones you'd typically add to any major or minor chords. It is best suited for B7(#5), B7(♭9), B13(♭9), and B7(#5♭9).

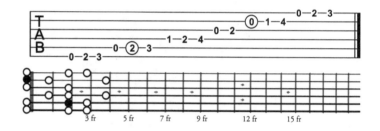

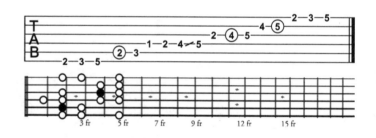

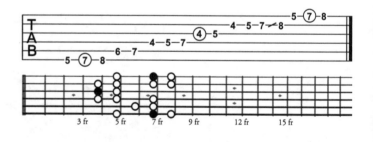

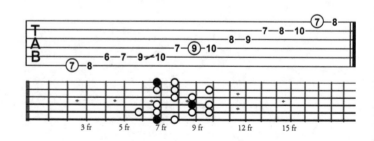

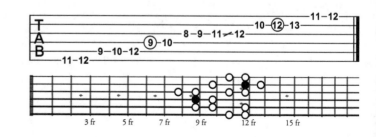

# B Jazz Melodic Minor

**SCALE DEGREES:** 1 2 ♭3 4 5 6 7
**SCALE TONES:** B C♯ D E F♯ G♯ A♯

There are actually two forms of the melodic minor scale, an ascending form (same as the scale shown here) and a descending form (same notes as the Aeolian mode). For purposes of improvisation, only the ascending version of the scale is used. The term "jazz minor" is used to describe this ascending only version of the scale.

While it is possible to use it over a power chord (B5), this scale is most often played over: Bm, Bm(add9), Bm6, Bm6/9, Bm(♯7), Bm(maj7), Bm(add9), Bm6/9(♯7), and Bm6/9(maj7).

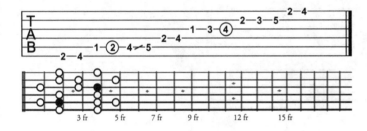

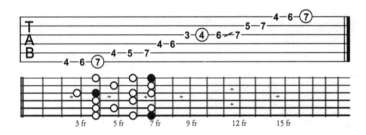

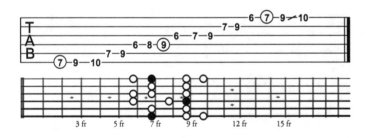

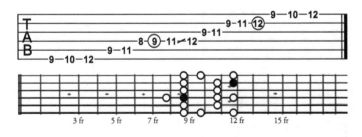

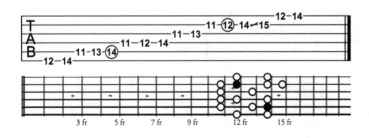

# B Lydian Dominant

**SCALE DEGREES:** 1 2 3 ♯4 5 6 ♭7
**SCALE TONES:** B C♯ D♯ E♯ F♯ G♯ A

Lydian Dominant is the fourth mode of the melodic minor scale. So B Lydian Dominant is the same as F♯ melodic minor played from B to B.

Like some of the other scales, this mode goes by a couple of other names: Mixolydian ♯4 and Lydian ♭7. It isn't used as a minor scale by improvisers since it is better suited to dominant chords that contain a ♭5 or ♯11. It is very similar to both the Lydian and Mixolydian modes as the alternate names suggest.

While it is possible to use it over a power chord (B5), this scale is most often played over: B7, B7(♭5), B7(♯11), B9, B9(♭5), B9(♯11), B13(♯11), and B13(♭5).

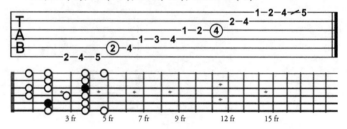

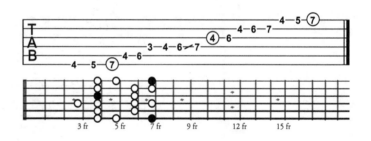

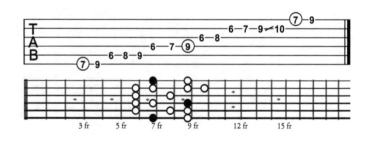

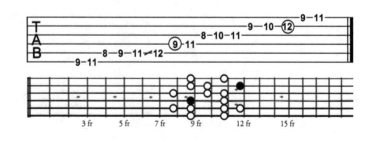

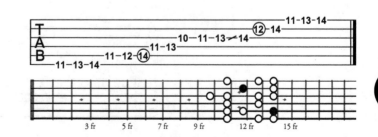

B

149

# B Super Locrian

**SCALE DEGREES:** 1 ♭2 ♭3 ♭4 ♭5 ♭6 ♭7
**SCALE TONES:** B C D E♭ F G A

Super Locrian is the seventh mode of the melodic minor scale. So B Super Locrian is the same as C melodic minor played from B to B.

The "diminished/whole-tone scale," and "altered scale" are two alternate names for this mode.

This mode contains all of the tension tones that can be absorbed in a dominant chord. These tones are the ♭5, ♯5, ♭9, and ♯9.

Use it over B7, B7(♭5), B7(♯5), B7(♭5♭9), B7(♭5♯9), B7(♯11), B7(♭9), B7(♯9), B13(♭9), and B13(♯9).

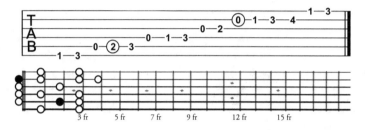

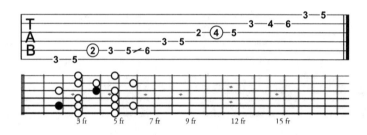

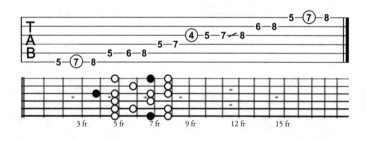

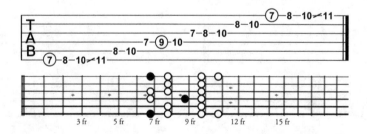

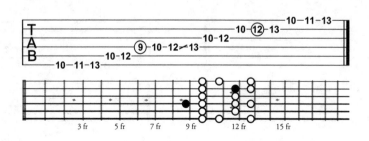

# B Diminished (whole-half)

**SCALE DEGREES:** 1  2  ♭3  4  ♭5  ♯5  6  7
**SCALE TONES:** B  C♯  D  E  F  F×  G♯  A♯

Sometimes called the symmetrical or fully diminished scale, this eight-note scale has some unusual traits. It is useful to understand how the scale is constructed. The primary notes of the scale are those that make up the diminished 7th chord: 1-♭3-♭5-♭♭7. The intervals that occur between these notes are all minor 3rds. The other four notes in this scale are located one half-step below each of these chord tones.

The symmetry in this scale lies in the basic building block of a whole-step followed by a half-step. This "cell" is repeated until the octave is reached.

This symmetry results in the fact that every third note can be considered the root note of the scale. The scale shown here will work with the Bdim7, Ddim7, Fdim7, and G♯dim7 chords. The grey notes in the scale patterns represent these alternate root tones. The scale can be started or ended on either the solid black notes or the grey notes.

Note that the scale pattern repeats itself every three frets, making it quite easy to play at any location on the fingerboard.

# B Diminished (half-whole)

**SCALE DEGREES:** 1  ♭2  ♭3  ♯3  ♯4  5  6  ♭7
**SCALE TONES:** B  C  D  D♯  E♯  F♯  G♯  A

Like the diminished scale (whole-half), this scale is symmetrical. It is the only mode possible in the diminished scale and it is exactly the same as the whole-half diminished scale, except it begins with a half-step instead of a whole-step. The basic building block consists of a half-step followed by a whole-step. This sequence repeats until the octave is reached.

All of this symmetry results in the fact that every third note can be considered the root note of the scale. The scale shown here will work with the B7, B7(♭9), B7(♯9), B7(♭5), B7(♯11), B13(♭9), B7(♭5♭9), and B7(♭5♯9) chords. The only altered dominant chords that don't work with this scale are the ones that contain a ♯5.

The diminished scales are the only eight note scales in common use. Most scales have seven different notes.

The grey notes in the scale patterns represent alternate root tones. The scale can be started or ended on either the solid black notes or the grey notes.

Note that the scale pattern repeats itself every three frets, making it quite easy to play at any location on the fingerboard. Just transpose either of these patterns up or down the fingerboard a distance of three frets.

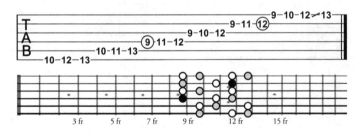

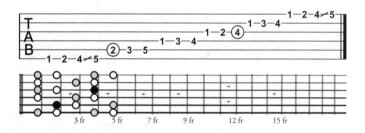

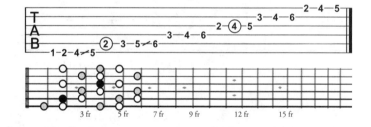

# B Major Pentatonic

SCALE DEGREES: 1 2 3 5 6
SCALE TONES: B C# D# F# G#

The major pentatonic scale only has five notes, but it is a scale that is very useful when working in folk, pop, country, and bluegrass styles. This scale avoids the possible dissonance contained in the standard major scale by eliminating the 4th and 7th scale degrees. It can be used over a power chord (B5) as well as Bmaj, B6, B6/9, B(add9), Bsus2, Bmaj7 and Bmaj9.

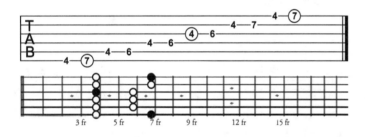

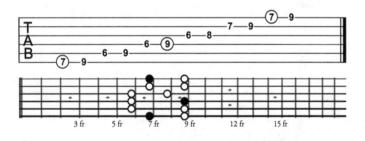

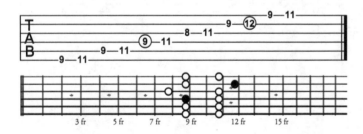

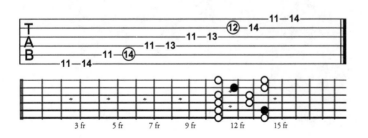

# B Minor Pentatonic

SCALE DEGREES: 1 b3 4 5 b7
SCALE TONES: B D E F# A

Like the major pentatonic, this scale only contains five notes and is often called the rock scale. It can be traced to the Aeolian (natural minor scale) with two notes removed, the 2nd and 6th.

This scale fits over the power chord (B5) as well as over Bm, Bm6, Bm7, Bm6/9, Bm(add9), Bm11, Bm7sus4, Bm13, B7, B9, and B7(#9). In general, use it when you want a rock sound, even if the chord is major.

Since this scale is very similar to the blues scale, they may be used in place of each other.

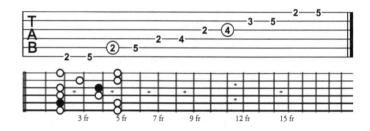

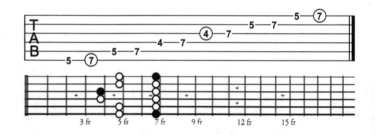

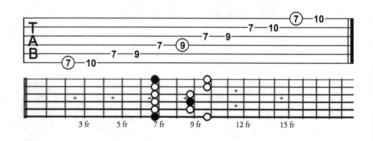

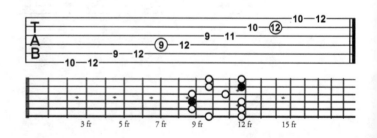

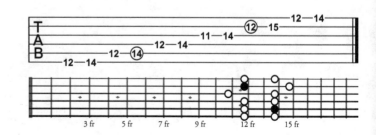

B

# B Blues

**SCALE DEGREES:** 1 ♭3 4 ♯4 5 ♭7
**SCALE TONES:** B D E E♯ F♯ A

This is a six-note scale and is really just a minor pentatonic with the addition of the ♯4.

Use this scale in the same places where you'd use the minor pentatonic, when you want a bluesy/rock effect.

This scale fits over the power chord (B5) as well as over a wide range of other chords in the minor and dominant categories. Try it over: Bm, Bm6, Bm7, Bm6/9, Bm(add9), Bm11, Bm7sus4, Bm13, B7, B9, and B7(♯9). It is even played over some major chords. Try it!

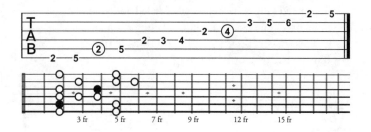

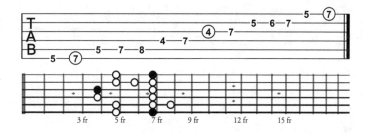

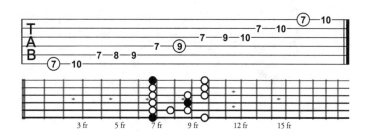

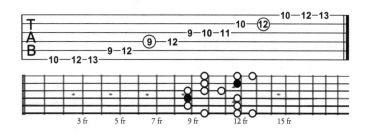

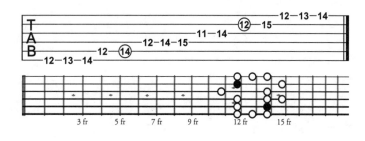

**B**

153

# B Whole Tone

**SCALE DEGREES:** 1  2  3  #4  #5  ♭7
**SCALE TONES:** B  C#  D#  E#  F×  A

This six-note scale is probably the easiest to finger of any in this book. What makes it so simple is the fact that the distance from one note to the next is always the same, a whole-step. Because of this symmetry, any note in the scale can actually be called the root. The black dots in these patterns represent B notes, but feel free to start and end on any of the tones in the scale.

Only two fingerings are needed to play this scale since any fingering can be moved up or down the neck in two-fret increments.

The sound of this scale is unlike any other in this book due to the lack of half-steps. This lack of half-steps makes the scale feel very unsettled and void of a tonic note. The feeling is akin to falling through space.

This scale works great with B7(#5), B9(#5), B7(♭5), B9(♭5), B13(♭5), or B13(#5).

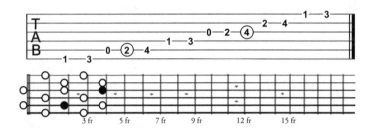

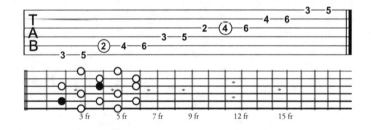